QUEEN ELIZABETH II

ABOVE: **The coronation procession unwinds; a souvenir scroll produced for the coronation of Queen Elizabeth II in 1953.**

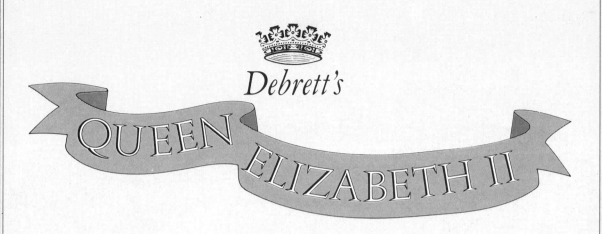

Debrett's

QUEEN ELIZABETH II

CHRISTOPHER WARWICK

Webb&Bower

EXETER, ENGLAND

Other books by Christopher Warwick

King George VI & Queen Elizabeth
Princess Margaret
Two Centuries of Royal Weddings

First published in Great Britain 1986 by
Webb & Bower (Publishers) Limited
9 Colleton Crescent, Exeter, Devon EX2 4BY

Designed by Peter Wrigley

Production by Nick Facer

British Library Cataloguing in Publication Data

Warwick, Christopher
    Debrett's Queen Elizabeth II : 60 glorious years.
    1. Elizabeth II, *Queen of Great Britain*
    2. Great Britain—Kings and rulers—Biography
    I. Title
    941.085′092′4   DA590

ISBN 0–86350–096–X

Typeset in Great Britain by Keyspools Ltd, Golborne, Lancashire

Printed and bound in Italy by New Interlitho Spa

CONTENTS

INTRODUCTION

'Elizabeth The Second, By The Grace of God,
of The United Kingdom of Great Britain
and Northern Ireland
and of Her Other Realms and Territories
Queen, Head of the Commonwealth,
Defender of the Faith.'

By these lofty-sounding titles—and there are others, such as Supreme Commander of the Armed Forces, Supreme Governor of the Church of England, and Lord High Admiral—is known an essentially modest and unassuming woman whose sixtieth birthday, on 21st April 1986, is commemorated within these pages.

This book has not been conceived so much as a biography, however, in the sense that it attempts a detailed or in-depth study, but more as a kind of royal kaleidoscope, snatching glimpses of some of the most colourful and, indeed, memorable, events that have occurred in the life—and during the reign—of Her Majesty The Queen.

LEFT: Her Majesty as Lord High Admiral, is piped aboard the aircraft carrier *Ark Royal* during the royal Jubilee visit to the Fleet at Spithead.

CHAPTER ONE
PORTRAIT OF A QUEEN

LEFT: Visiting Hackney, the Queen receives a warm welcome from local residents.

For more than a century the Balmoral estate on Royal Deeside in the Highlands of Scotland has been beloved of successive generations of the royal family. To Queen Victoria, Balmoral was ever 'This Dear Paradise'. Indeed, there was little about it that failed to enthrall her. The densely wooded hillsides—over which, to the south, towers Lochnagar—reminded her of the Prince Consort's adored Thuringian Woods. As a gifted painter she captured the changing moods and colours of the landscape in watercolours; she built hut-like cottages or cabins by the edge of the lochs where she and her 'dearest Albert' could rest and take refreshment and, stone by stone, built cairns whenever and wherever the mood took her to mark special occasions or anniversaries. She delighted in the forthright manner of the people and, during the 1840s and 1850s, she and Prince Albert took an equal delight in trekking for miles—frequently on horseback and incognito—through the surrounding countryside. Together they entered enthusiastically into the spirit of local activities, such as the annual Braemar Games, and shared their pleasures with friends and relations who joined the royal shooting, stalking and fishing parties. For Queen Victoria herself there was also a welcome sense of remoteness from the more onerous reminders of her official role as sovereign.

Contented images such as these thoughts present do not belong specifically or peculiarly to the reign of Victoria. In fact the pattern of royal family life at Balmoral today is as familiar as it was a century ago. To the present Queen and her family Balmoral holds much the same magic, much the same allure, as that which first captivated Elizabeth II's great-great-grandmother and persuaded her to build a private residence of her own—in the 'Scotch Baronial' style—where she and her consort might find their own kind of *Gemütlichkeit* ('cosiness'). Little has changed at Balmoral Castle since those days and throughout the house there are innumerable reminders of Victoria and Albert, not least the white and gold wallpaper on the walls of the staircase printed with the Queen's cipher, and William Theed's statue of the Prince Consort which still stands near the foot of the main stairs leading off the ground-floor gallery.

The royal family's annual migration invariably begins, as it always has, in early August. Once upon a time the Queen would journey overnight aboard the maroon-painted royal train from King's Cross in London to its small counterpart at Ballater. From there the remainder of the journey to Balmoral would be undertaken by car. Since the

smaller station's closure, however, the Queen has sailed from South-ampton aboard the royal yacht *Britannia* up the west coast of Britain. Towards the end of the cruise, the royal yacht puts into Scrabster Harbour for the now traditional luncheon appointment with Queen Elizabeth The Queen Mother, and there, on the quayside as the royal barge approaches, Her Majesty waits to greet her daughter.

At Balmoral, second only to Sandringham in the Queen's affec-tions, Her Majesty is able to loosen if not entirely throw off, the grand mantle of sovereignty and become, as one who knows her well has put it, 'a housewife-manqué'. For it is in the relative seclusion of her highland estate that the Queen has the opportunity to indulge in the kind of small pleasures that her estimated one billion subjects, dispersed across the globe, take very much for granted. Chief among them is her love of picnics, *al fresco* by the edge of Loch Muick, or in the shade of her newest log-cabin.

On such occasions the Queen insists on laying out the tables personally and brewing the tea from a kettle firmly placed in front of her. Pages and footmen may indeed load up the land-rovers, but they are banished from the royal presence when it comes to tea-time. This is, in fact, the closest Queen Elizabeth II can ever come to being 'ordinary'. It is the closest she will ever be in spirit to the habits and routines of untold millions of women—wives and mothers—the world over.

There is, of course, an element of 'let's pretend' about this kind of royal ritual, neatly summed up by the Queen Mother during the Balmoral sojourn of 1984. No grouse—and therefore no shooting parties—meant that the Queen put off her usual houseguests and instead invited individual friends and relations to stay for a few days at the castle. On one particularly fine afternoon that summer, as she sat in the drawing-room chatting to her cousin Lady Elizabeth Shakerley, her husband Sir Geoffrey, and her mother, the Queen exclaimed contentedly 'Goodness, what a lovely day it is,' and suggested, 'Why don't we have tea in the log-cabin?' Breaking off for a moment's thought, she then added, 'Oh! I don't think I have the keys.' At that point the Queen Mother opened her arms in a typical gesture and, teasing her daughter, remarked, 'But darling, all *you* have to say is "Open Sesame"!'

Playfully delivered the Queen Mother's remark nevertheless underlines the simple truth about the *extra*ordinary nature of the lives members of the royal family—and in particular the Queen herself—

have always led. Long ago when he was still Duke of York, King George VI is on record as having said that he was only a very ordinary man, when he was allowed to be one. He was mistaken. For a system such as ours prevents royal figures from being 'ordinary'. It does not, however, prevent them from being *human*, and therein lies a very subtle, but quite distinct, difference.

Sixty years ago, the child who was to become Queen Elizabeth II was born into a family which stood at the very apex of a society which sharply divided and compartmentalized the population into three classes, within which they were again sub-divided into levels. More than half a century later, a still evolving sense of egalitarianism has done much to neutralize the rigidity of the class system. Yet while 'paupers' may easily rub shoulders with peers, the 'mystique' or the 'sanctity' of monarchy has, to all intents and purposes, remained intact. And it is precisely because the familiar persona of monarchy has been so carefully preserved that the very idea that it is represented by 'ordinary' people is invalidated. On the whole, however, it is still true to say that most people, no matter how illogically, seem to want to imagine members of the royal family as both semi-mystical, yet quite 'ordinary'. Almost ten years ago, at the time of the Queen's Silver Jubilee in 1977, Robert Lacey—author of *Majesty—Elizabeth II and the House of Windsor*—raised a very similar issue.

'Majesty in [the Queen's] terms', he wrote, 'is the majesty of the common man—and she also embodies the hope that at the centre of the vast, impersonal machinery of the modern state might lie an ordinary human being, living and breathing like everyone else.' It is a fascinating conundrum—what is real and what is unreal? Where is the separating line between the predictability of unspectacular royal routine and the masquerade coloured by magical illusion? Thus in her official capacity, the Queen has to maintain a careful balancing act, negotiating each step that is made along a symbolic tightrope. As sovereign she must remain in touch with the lives of her subjects, whilst allowing the institution she represents to remain one step removed. At the same time she must never lose sight of herself—as an individual and as a human.

At sixty the Queen enjoys greater confidence in herself, both as a person and as a sovereign, than at almost any other time in her life. As her children Charles, Anne, Andrew and Edward were growing up,

Seated in St Edward's Choir, the Queen solemnly awaits the act of Anointing. Behind Her Majesty the canopy of Cloth-of-Gold is borne forward.

and particularly once the Prince of Wales had reached adulthood, dynastic considerations weighed heavily on the Queen's mind, to the extent that many were of the opinion that she was unnecessarily preoccupied with the question of the monarchy's survival after her.

Prince Charles's eventual marriage to Lady Diana Spencer, at the age of thirty-two, and moreover the subsequent births of his sons William and Henry, released the Queen from further anxiety. Almost immediately, as members of her family confirm, Her Majesty seemed to become more relaxed, much calmer, and yet more willing to counsel and assist those close to her, especially at times of trouble.

'In private the Queen has become more human', the author was told. 'She has come to understand people so much better and she *wants* to know about their lives. In the past she has been very badly informed about the minutiae of family life and what has been going on around her in general, She realizes that, because she is *The Queen*, a good deal has been kept away from her. But she is terribly interested in the small everyday things. They *do* matter to her.'

One but by no means isolated or exceptional example of the Queen's concern for others—and in this case for a total stranger—recently came to light on the other side of the Atlantic. The story told of an aged British-born woman's desire to spend her last days in England. Ninety-nine-year-old Mary Armstrong had gone to the United States more than sixty years earlier where she had married a fellow Briton. A resident of Los Angeles in her later years, Mrs Armstrong petitioned the British consulate to be permitted to return permanently to England. To her dismay she had been told that the most she could hope for was a visitor's visa, enabling her to spend a maximum period of six months in Britain.

'I was born and raised in England, and I want to die in England', she protested and promptly wrote to the Queen. Not long afterwards, as she packed her cases, Mrs Armstrong proclaimed triumphantly, 'It pays to go to the top', and pointed to a letter from Buckingham Palace in which she was informed that the Queen had instructed the Home Office to issue a 'Certificate of Entitlement' enabling her to return to England.

Yet closer to home *The Times* ran an entertaining 'Diary' story in March 1985 which illustrates the interest Her Majesty takes in even the less close branches of her own family. Entitled *Gentleman of Letters*, it read:

'A close relative of the Queen tells me a marvellous story about one of the monarch's relations, who left a prestigious City job some years ago to become a recluse on the west coast of Scotland. The man has taken his hermit existence to heart and refuses to answer a single letter. As a result a room in his home has a huge pile of un-opened correspondence in the centre. The Queen, faintly irked that her letters are never answered, but highly tickled by her eccentric relation, was sailing down the west coast in *Britannia* when she suddenly ordered her captain to drop anchor. Someone was duly dispatched to fetch the recluse who, according to my source, was found washing his socks on the rocks. Sadly, my informant will not be drawn on the man's identity.'

At the beginning of her reign the Queen was generally regarded as a rather diffident and serious young woman. Like the first Elizabeth, Henry VIII's autocratic and awe-inspiring daughter 'Gloriana', King George VI's daughter came to the throne at the age of twenty-five. Her accession gave rise to endless euphoric babble and full-blown rhetoric, proclaiming the dawn of a new and glorious Elizabethan Age. The press constantly reminded the nation that Britain had always been at its greatest under its queens regnant and cited Tudor might and Victorian empire-building as the most obvious examples. Yet when such sentiments simmered down and the flag-waving became a memory, more critical voices were raised, but not simply about the monarchy as a whole.

In 1957 John Grigg, then Lord Altrincham, announced that the Queen's personality as 'conveyed by the utterances which are put into her mouth is that of a priggish schoolgirl, captain of the hockey team, a prefect and a recent candidate for confirmation'. The same year Malcom Muggeridge published an article which was construed more as an attack on the Queen than on the system and caused a wild furore of indignation. All the same Muggeridge had made a bitingly true statement when he said, 'It is duchesses not shop assistants who find the Queen dowdy, frumpish and banal. The appeal of the monarchy is to the gallery rather than to the stalls . . .'. Later the playwright John Osborne, the 'Angry Young Man' of the British theatre during the 1950s, declared royalty to be 'a gold filling in a mouth full of decay'.

Almost thirty years later the Queen, as a person, is very rarely criticized; the monarchy, though it has always been open to criticism—and doubtless always will be for as long as it survives— would appear less vulnerable to vehement attack. Much of the credit

The Queen and Prince Philip entertained Marshal Tito to lunch at Buckingham Palace in
March 1953. With them in the Picture Gallery are the Queen Mother and Princess Margaret.

for this is due to the attitudes of the Queen herself. For over the past fifteen years or so, she has successfully established a more comfortable style for her family and her successors to follow.

One lady-in-waiting recently said that, nowadays, the Queen 'thoroughly enjoys every minute of her life'. Taken at face value the reasons behind such a statement are perfectly clear. It is, however, a sweeping assertion, when we know that much in the Queen's private life has been far from perfect. What is true is that Elizabeth II has learned well the lessons experience and maturity have taught her and today, especially, she has every reason to reflect on her life's achievements with satisfaction and, perhaps, a comfortable sense of fulfilment.

Since the days of George III, royal history has revealed that most of Britain's sovereigns have preferred to look no further than 'the hearth' for private contentment. Certainly during the earlier part of this century George V and Queen Mary and, later, George VI and Queen Elizabeth did not aspire to anything grander. The same is equally true of the present Queen. Unlike the Prince of Wales and the Duke and Duchess of Kent, she is not much attracted to the opera or, like her sister, to the ballet. Outside official visits she is not a renowned theatre-goer and in private seldom entertains on a particularly lavish scale. The bright, somewhat superficial lights of showbusiness have never beckoned to her in the same way that they have captivated Princess Margaret, nor has she ever associated herself with society's so-called 'beautiful people', or the sun-drenched playgrounds of the idle rich. In short Queen Elizabeth II is a woman of comparatively simple and unpretentious tastes and interests.

There can be no doubt that had she been given a choice, the Queen would have exchanged her royal life at birth for one which would have allowed her to enjoy an anonymous existence as a countrywoman, immersed in country pursuits, and, indeed, she has admitted as much on more than one occasion.

Horses are, perhaps, the greatest love of the Queen's life. She is as much at home riding purely for pleasure as she is studying form at Epsom or Royal Ascot. And she is never more contented than when, with the eye of an expert, she watches one of her race horses being put through its paces or simply, as an observer, attending such annual events as the Badminton Horse Trials or the Royal Windsor Horse Show. Even in the privacy of her apartments at Buckingham Palace and Windsor Castle, the occasional sound of daytime television

probably means that the Queen is avidly watching a video-recording of a race she was unable to attend—especially true of meetings in which her own horses have been competing.

Dogs, too, have their place in the Queen's life. From childhood she has been deeply attached to corgis and, in recent years, the smaller 'dorki'—a cross between a corgi and a dachshund—has become almost as popular within the immediate royal family. There is in fact an amusing story of a startled footman gasping '*Your Majesty*!' in utter disbelief one day when he came across the Queen and Princess Margaret down on all fours attempting to persuade one of the Queen's corgis to take an interest in the Princess's dachshund 'Pippin'. Gun dogs are also favourites with the Queen; so much so, that she regularly takes a hand in helping to train them personally.

Like all true animal lovers the world over, the Queen enjoys establishing close relationships with all her dogs as individual personalities and when, not so long ago, one of them became seriously ill and had to be destroyed, the Queen insisted on cradling him in her arms quite literally to the very end.

It might accurately be said that Her Majesty's attachment to her animals is made stronger by the fact that, in her personal friendships, she has no choice but to exercise the utmost care. Other members of the royal family may be in a position to extend the hand of friendship with more freedom, embracing individuals from almost every walk of life. The Queen, however, cannot afford to indulge in the same kind of luxury. Loyalty and total discretion are the foundations on which a friendship with the sovereign are founded. Thus the Queen cannot claim more than, let us say, a handful of close and trusted friends, people with whom she can properly relax and exchange opinions and confidences, in the sure knowledge that they will never be repeated.

Though given what most of us would regard as a framework of considerable limitations in which to operate, it would be a grave mistake to imagine that the *de*humanizing aspects of the Queen's position restrict her overall 'humanness' as a person. She has, for example, a ready sense of humour and an appealing joke will be greeted with what one of her cousins describes as 'a very young laugh', making her 'look and sound just like a girl once more'. Another has said, in similar vein, 'the Queen is a great giggler, but not like some of us who go on and on and never seem to know when to stop'.

On the other side of the coin—as one who has known her well for many years remarked—'The Queen actually spends more time alone

than you would think.' It is then that she enjoys tackling such everyday pastimes as jig-saw puzzles or simply watching television, programmes ranging from the most serious documentary to the most glib soap-opera. A friend has said, 'If you call when the Queen is watching *Coronation Street*, you can hardly get a sensible word out of her.'

In Aden during the coronation tour the Queen is clearly amused by the outfit worn by a member of the Aden Executive, particularly by the skirt he wears with woollen socks and lace-up shoes.

In company Her Majesty 'absolutely sparkles' as an amusing and entertaining conversationalist, her hands gesticulating in a continental way, all the while. Over dinner everybody is expected to join in the cross-talk, not waiting to be addressed by the Queen first as protocol used to demand. Beforehand, sipping a pre-prandial dry martini, a gin

and tonic or a gin and dubonnet, Her Majesty enjoys mingling informally and prefers to be regarded simply as one of the guests. But woe-betide anybody who takes the Queen's friendliness as a signal for a familiar remark. For like her sister, Princess Margaret, the Queen will freeze the 'offender' with a firm, steady stare, wearing what has been called her 'Miss Piggy' face or, as one of her late great-aunts used to put it, her 'chinless look'.

The almost 'royal' gift of mimicry, shared by the Queen, her mother and her sister, is a talent that is often remarked upon by those who have heard it. Of the three, however, it has been said that the Queen's 'act' is the sharpest and most hilarious, not only reflecting her dry wit but also her keenly observant eye. Card games, such as 'Racing Demon', a favourite since childhood, might—at a house-party—be followed by charades. No doubt allied to some extent to her love of amateur theatricals, nurtured at Windsor during the war, the Queen ropes her guests into these games and as one once put it, 'How can you refuse the Queen, even if you do feel a bloody fool?' Fools, as it happens, are not suffered gladly by any member of the royal family and least of all by the Queen herself. Although broad-minded, she does not care for smutty or malicious gossip, but a risqué joke is almost sure to amuse. Unfortunately the Queen's highly developed sense of humour and her equally keen sense of fun aren't often seen by the public at large. But it frequently emerges even in the midst of the most formal engagement. Joining the line-up of prime ministers before a reception during the Commonwealth Conference in Zambia in 1982, the Queen settled herself on a small gilt chair, placed her glittering evening bag on her lap, crossed her silver-shoed feet at the ankles (as all royal ladies are taught to do) and joked with cameramen and film crews, 'There. Do we look nice—we're supposed to'. A year later, during their rain-sodden visit to the United States, the Queen and Prince Philip again posed for formal photographs, this time with President Reagan and his wife Nancy.

'Before you arrived, we had perfect weather', the President quipped. 'You must have brought the rain with you.'

'Oh, that's very nice I must say. Thanks very much', the Queen responded, wearing an almost deadpan expression.

On yet another occasion, Hugh Scanlon of the Trades Union Congress told how the Queen helped him overcome a moment of embarrassment during a luncheon party at Buckingham Palace. His was the misfortune, in such august company, to spear a piece of roast

potato, only to watch it slip off his plate onto the floor. The Queen may never have noticed had it not been for one of her corgis. Hoping for a tasty morsel it moved away from her chair towards the fallen vegetable, gave it a sniff and then retreated. 'It's not your day, Mr Scanlon, is it?', the Queen laughed.

Very rarely has the monarchy and all its ramifications been thoroughly scrutinized. Indeed, the last time a book was published on the subject was in 1970. Then, in his neatly investigative and highly entertaining study, *The Reality of Monarchy*, still one of the best 'royal' books ever to have been written, Andrew Duncan observed, 'It is one of the curious phenomena of the late twentieth century that such an eccentric institution can not only survive, but apparently thrive. Millions of the Queen's gloom-laden subjects, wincing with all the rivetingly documented withdrawal symptoms of power, sink comfortably into the past, raise their glasses, and say, "Well, thank God we've got her".'

A decade and a half later, very little has changed, save, perhaps, that people's attitudes have been tempered still further by disillusionment and cynicism. Yet, Andrew Duncan went on, 'If nothing else, the British are world champions at the Monarchy game, producing competitors who are less drab than the Dutch, less pompous than the Scandinavians, and more sophisticated than the most devious President.'

In the recent past, though its continuing existence cannot be said to have come under any serious threat, the monarchy encountered something of a watershed during the second half of the 1960s. On a national, and as other countries followed our lead, international, level there hadn't been a more go-ahead, even revolutionary, period this century. In almost every respect the population, and especially the young, took every advantage of the opportunities the times offered to enjoy a new sense of liberation—a freedom both of thought and expression.

During that period 'one of the Queen's most influential religious advisers' who spoke to Andrew Duncan considered the monarchy to be 'dead from the neck up', but added that it stood poised to regain its popularity once more. Within the next few years the Crown, as represented by the more immediate members of the royal family— notably the young Prince of Wales and his fashion-conscious sister Princess Anne, at that time newcomers to the royal stage—did reclaim

its popular standing, and at an increasingly steady pace. Influenced by the late Lord Mountbatten, Prince Philip's uncle and a great friend, the Queen allowed a television film—called *Royal Family*—to be made, and when shown it commanded an avid audience that was counted in millions. From then on it seemed as if the Queen became more conscious of the need to keep the nation more closely in touch with the 'domestic' side of royal family life, and thus the media was permitted greater access and far better facilities than had ever been known before.

As a further bonus the Queen instituted the novelty of the 'walkabout' while touring New Zealand in 1970, and despite the vast security loopholes that have developed since then, Her Majesty remains adamant that she must still see and be seen by the public. Even in view of incidents that occurred during the early 1980s the Queen refuses to yield to more conspicuous protection, all of which says an enormous amount for the strength of her personal level of bravery and courage.

It is not only the vulnerability of the Queen's position—from a safety angle—that makes hers the least enviable of public roles, but the sheer weight of responsibility that falls to the sovereign as to no other member of the royal family. In the words of the late Sir Arthur Bryant, 'The Queen does not only symbolize and help promote the unity of her people, she serves to remind them of their ideals. She represents in her person and family life, and in her dedication to her public duties, the abiding virtues of hearth, home and service on the foundations of which society rests.'

Perhaps to some extent all that might seem a little too fanciful, especially when considering the largely unsatisfactory plight of society today. But at least the ideology remains as valid and optimistic as it ever was. Beyond doubt, the Queen has certainly always worked to 'promote' the unity and the interests of 'her people', both at home and abroad.

At all events Britain has in its monarchy an invaluable safety mechanism built into the 'system'; one which provides a focus for people's loyalty and patriotic emotions, free from the entreaties and exhortations of party politics. As a constitutional sovereign, the Queen is officially apolitical and therefore above such things. Indeed, as Lord Hailsham once put it, 'Our monarchy is the one part of our constitution which is still working as it was designed to do.'

Under the constitution the sovereign is, of course, virtually

powerless, save for her immense personal influence and a certain authority invested in her by Parliament. Yet the Queen still remains an essential instrument of government. Without royal assent Parliament could not be summoned or its politics become law; taxes could not be levied, nor any minister, judge, magistrate, officer of the armed services, ambassador or bishop be appointed. Moreover, without royal assent, no promotion in public service, no honour or pardon could be deemed valid. Theoretically the Queen could bring the machinery of government—all of which operates in her name—to a grinding halt. In reality the Queen would not dare to exercise the Royal Prerogative in so extreme a manner—unless it was necessary to preserve the peace of the realm.

According to the constitution—and we are reminded of this by Walter Bagehot's scholarly work which is still a constant source of reference—the sovereign has three specific rights. They are the right to be consulted, the right to encourage and the right to warn. 'A king of great sense and sagacity would want no others', wrote Bagehot. 'He would find that his having no others would enable him to use these with singular effect. A wise king would gradually acquire a fund of knowledge and experience which few ministers could rival.'

Elizabeth II is, in fact, living proof of all that Bagehot advocated, and it is worth noting that none of her prime ministers—Winston Churchill, Anthony Eden, Harold Macmillan, Alec Douglas-Home, Harold Wilson, Edward Heath, James Callaghan or Margaret Thatcher—has failed to be impressed by the Queen's skills in the delicate craft of statesmanship. Some of her relationships with her prime ministers have, understandably, been more cordial than others, but two she particularly enjoyed meeting were Sir Winston Churchill (because his audiences with her were 'always such fun') and Harold Wilson who, at the end of his premiership, said, 'If we in Britain had been governed for hundreds of years by a presidential system, the best constitutional innovation for modern times would be to invent a sovereign . . .'. Of the Queen herself, Sir Harold (now Lord) Wilson went on, 'You realize very quickly that she is a unique repository of knowledge . . . and what emerges is a combination of experience, very hard work, a good memory and good judgement—both about things and about people.'

A few years later, in conversation with the Countess of Longford, the eminent historian and biographer, former prime minister James Callaghan said, 'One gets a great deal of friendliness. And Prime

Ministers also get a great deal of understanding of their problems—without the Queen sharing them, since she is outside politics. I think she weighs them up, but doesn't often offer advice. . . . Of course she may have hinted at things, but only on the rarest occasions do I remember her ever saying, "Why don't you do this, that or the other?" She is pretty detached on all that. But she's very interested in the political side—who's going up and who's going down.'

On the subject of domestic politics Mr Callaghan had this to say: 'The Queen has a deep sense of duty and responsibility in this area. . . . If her Prime Minister liked to give the Queen information . . . about certain political characters, she would listen very attentively, for she has a real understanding of the value of a constitutional monarchy. I think she is absolutely right to be on the alert. I think the prestige of the monarchy could deteriorate if she didn't work so hard at it. Every monarch makes his or her niche in people's minds and hearts, and this Queen has done that.'

Successive Commonwealth premiers have also been equally gratified by the Queen's commitment to that body of nations over which, as Head, she officially presides. In her Christmas Day broadcast of 1953, Her Majesty said, 'The Commonwealth bears no resemblance to the empires of the past. It is an entirely new conception . . . an equal partnership of nations and races.' Although no longer quite so 'new' in concept, it is nevertheless something to which the Queen remains devoted, and while the inevitable winds of change may echo dissenting voices, its Head vigorously continues to champion its cause, its validity and its continuation. It is certainly no secret that the Queen takes a dim view over ministerial interference in her work as Head of the Commonwealth, and in 1979, for example, Her Majesty made her displeasure known to Mrs Thatcher when the Prime Minister—who did not intend to cancel her own visit—suggested to the Queen that she might think twice before attending the Commonwealth conference in Lusaka that July.

It was of course true that, in 1979, Her Majesty's visit was considered a high-risk operation, exacerbated by the acceleration of guerilla tactics on the Rhodesian border. But the Queen knew all about the dangers and was prepared for a tough mission, one in which only she could possibly help diffuse a tense situation. Rifts in Africa and the breakdown of diplomatic relations were nothing new. This time, though, there was a particular intensity about the differences of those on what had been described as the Zimbabwe–Rhodesia 'battlefront',

ABOVE: The State Visit to the United States: Her Majesty on the steps of the Capitol.

TOP RIGHT: Her Majesty addresses the highest assembly in the land in the House of Lords during the State Opening of Parliament.

TOP CENTRE RIGHT: During his official visit to Britain in 1982 the Queen was accompanied by the US President, Ronald Reagan, when she went out riding in the grounds of Windsor Castle.

TOP FAR RIGHT: The Queen's tour of the Gulf States was possibly the most important of all the State Visits she has undertaken during her reign. The Queen is seen with the Sultan of Oman.

RIGHT: 'Do we look nice—we're supposed to', Her Majesty joked with newsmen covering the Commonwealth Conference in Zambia as she joined the line up of premiers, including Britain's Margaret Thatcher, for a formal group portrait.

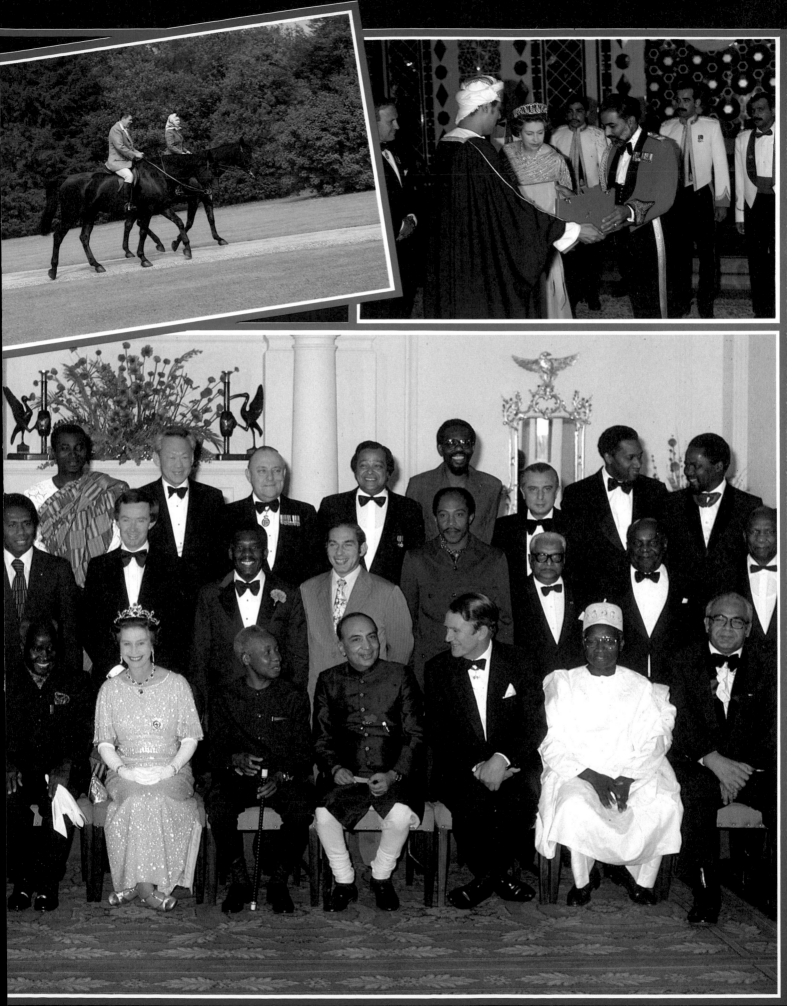

RIGHT: Dressed in the robe of Sovereign of the Order of St Michael and St George, the Queen leaves St Paul's Cathedral, attended by a page-of-honour and followed by her Mistress of the Robes, the Duchess of Grafton.

BELOW: Her Majesty posing with The Queen's Company of the Grenadier Guards.

During the epic coronation tour of the Commonwealth, 1953/54,
the Queen opened Parliament in Wellington, New Zealand.

and there was a strong chance of hostile 'activity' during the Queen's visit.

As Head the Queen does not participate in the meetings of Commonwealth leaders. But she does receive them all individually in a constant succession of 'one-to-one' audiences, listening intently and offering well-reasoned advice and guidance on issues with which she is always fully conversant. Therein lies the power and the success of her Commonwealth missions. In Lusaka she sat all day in a sparsely furnished study, locked in earnest discussion with leader after leader. By the time she finally headed for home, harmony had been re-established and settlements arranged. High diplomacy had taken the Queen to Kenya, Tanzania, Malawi, Botswana and Zambia, covering a distance of 15,000 miles in seventeen days. Nobody had been overlooked and nothing had been forgotten.

Amid all the tension, however, there were several light moments. In Botswana, for instance, one village chief, when told that the Queen was about to visit him, asked, 'Oh, is that Queen Victoria?' When he was told no, unfortunately she was now dead, the chief asked sniffily, 'Well then, why weren't we invited to the funeral?' And as the Queen's aircraft took off for London, she looked down on a scene of waving crowds, calling in amusing unison, 'Bye bye, Queenie!'

As Queen, not only of England, Scotland, Wales and Northern Ireland, but of ten other countries—from Canada to the Antipodes—and as Head of the Commonwealth, overseas visits naturally form a major part of Elizabeth II's official function. As a result, she has achieved the distinction of being the most widely travelled of all British sovereigns. Indeed, during the first twenty-five years of her reign, the Queen had undertaken forty-eight overseas visits (the current total stands at seventy-four) and had travelled 471,666 miles.

The first of her tours as Queen was the epic coronation tour of the Commonwealth which began in November 1953 and ended six months and 43,618 miles later in May 1954. This tour included formal visits to New Zealand, Australia, Jamaica, Panama, Fiji, Tonga, Sri Lanka (then Ceylon), Uganda, Malta and Gibraltar. The impact of Her Majesty's first tour was, of course, considerable. Yet in retrospect it was a gruelling and almost inhuman task to demand of a young wife and mother. When she departed Elizabeth II was twenty-six years old and had been Queen for less than two years. In that time she had had to cope not only with the myriad changes that becoming sovereign had made to her life, but had to adjust to the volume of duties which

ABOVE: **The Queen and the Duke of Edinburgh in Ceylon, 1954.**

TOP: **Applauded by local children the Queen leaves the church of St Michael
and All Angels during her visit to Ceylon, now Sri Lanka.**

ABOVE: Aboard the new Australian Navy flagship *Vengeance*, sailors were seen in formation on the flight-deck in exact facsimile of the Queen's signature 'Elizabeth R'.

RIGHT: Her Majesty knighting Sir William Goodfellow in Auckland. To the Queen's right is the royal equerry who, as the 8th Earl Spencer, was to become the Prince of Wales's father-in-law twenty-seven years later.

devolved upon her. Moreover, her accession had necessitated lengthy preparations for the ritual of her coronation as well as a succession of major events, such as the Spithead Review, all of which had only just been completed before she was required to embark on the most strenuous of all her royal tours.

One of the Queen's most diplomatically successful visits in recent years was that which she paid to the Federal Republic of Germany in 1978, before which the German Chancellor—Herr Schmidt—had made it perfectly clear that he considered the prospect of this second State Visit by the Queen of England, a bore. Her first had occurred during May 1965. In advance of Her Majesty's arrival Schmidt had warned that he would not be available to accompany the royal party to each engagement or public appearance. Yet, as this second visit

became every bit as successful and popular as the first, the Chancellor unexpectedly turned up time and time again.

In the past, too, Her Majesty has invariably steered clear of making speeches too heavily laden with political overtones. Not so today. In fact at the Blue Church in West Berlin, the Queen told her audience, 'My soldiers and men stationed in Berlin embody the British commitment to defend your freedom for as long as need be, till the division in Europe—and in your city—can be healed.' The Queen's visit to the United States two years before had proved another *tour de force* of diplomatic as well as personal strength. 'I speak to you as the direct descendant of George III', she said in her first speech of the tour. 'He was the last crowned sovereign to rule in this country.' Later on. when she presented the new six-ton Bicentennial Bell, cast in the foundry in Whitechapel (a part of London's East End) where the original Liberty Bell had been produced, the Queen said, 'Britain should celebrate Independence Day as much as America in sincere gratitude to the founding fathers of this great republic for teaching Britain a very valuable lesson. We lost the American colonies because we lacked the statesmanship to know the right time and the manner of yielding what was impossible to keep.

'In the following 150 years we learned to keep more closely to the principles of Magna Carta which have been the common heritage of both our countries. We learned to respect the right of others to govern themselves in their own way.'

The right of others to govern themselves was extended in 1982 to a country of which Elizabeth II herself was still Queen—Canada. At an open-air ceremony on Ottawa's rain-drenched Parliament Hill, on 19th April that year, the Queen proclaimed the new Canadian Constitution and the premier, Pierre Trudeau, announced joyfully that the last colonial link with Britain had been severed.

In the same year that the Queen paid State Visits to Denmark (as the guest of her distant cousin Queen Margrethe), to Tanzania, Malawi, Botswana and Zambia, and was formally entertained at the Elysée Palace in Paris following her private visits to Beaune and the châteaux of the Loire, so Her Majesty also undertook one of the most colourful and important journeys of her entire reign—east to the Gulf. The year was 1979 and that February she paid State Visits to Saudi Arabia, Kuwait, Bahrain, Qatar, the United Arab Emirates and Oman. There

were scenes to dazzle and impress any eyes, even those of so seasoned a traveller as the Queen. She was laden with £1 million-worth of exotic gifts—gold, silver, diamonds, sapphires, rubies, pearls—and in Saudi Arabia, as a woman in a man's world, she was regarded as an 'Honorary Gentleman' and frequently referred to as 'He' or 'Him'. King Khaled had never entertained a female sovereign before and points of protocol were very carefully scrutinized on both sides well beforehand. To have given offence, no matter how unintentionally, would have been to damage British trade relations and that, after all, was what this tour was all about.

One concession to the Queen's sex that could not be made, however, was the way in which she dressed and, at least whenever the king himself was present, Her Majesty and her ladies-in-waiting, on this occasion the Duchess of Grafton, Mistress of the Robes, and Lady Susan Hussey, had to appear in long dresses which did not reveal backs, necks, elbows or ankles.

As a rule the Queen's dress-sense has met frequent and, more often than not, quite justified criticism. The talents of such designers as Ian Thomas (successor to the late Sir Norman Hartnell, who dressed royal ladies for over forty years) and Hardy Amies, are rarely seen to best advantage in the predictably uninspiring outfits chosen by their most exalted client. But in the Gulf fashion correspondents waited eagerly to describe the royal wardrobe.

As expected the long-sleeved, full-skirted outfits that were to be shortened and worn over again back at home attracted most interest, and in Riyadh, as the Queen alighted gracefully from that most graceful of all aircraft, Concorde, all eyes were focused on the historic meeting between Britain's 'Honorary Gentleman', covered from head to foot in sapphire blue, and the tall, black-robed king who guided her to the airport's VIP lounge and her first welcoming cup of minted coffee. Ahead of the Queen and the Duke of Edinburgh lay a twenty-one-day programme of events which promised more than a mere dash of exotica and a fresh departure from the usual and rather unexciting routine of overseas visits.

At its close nobody was left in any doubt about the friendships the Queen had helped cement or the thriving business avenues that had been widened still further between the oil-rich countries of the East and their eager customer in the West. Yet if the Queen had skilfully accomplished long and exhausting visits to six countries with great tact and diplomacy, and had left each of her hosts charmed beyond

The Queen's patience began to wear thin when the King of Morocco
kept her waiting for more than three hours in the desert sun.

expectations, she needed every last ounce of forebearance at her
command, some twenty months later, when coping with the rigours of
what proved to be her most vexatious State Visit yet—to Morocco.

In October 1980, having already visited Switzerland in April and
Australia in May, the Queen set out on tours of Italy—which included
her first State Visit to the Vatican and Pope John Paul II—Tunisia and
Algeria, winding up her programme in the arid desert kingdom of
King Hassan. It was, nearly everybody agreed, an invitation that
should never have been accepted. Comparatively little was gained
from it and both the Queen and Prince Philip found themselves
repeatedly subjected to the ill-mannered and cavalier behaviour of the
despotic Moroccan ruler.

Advance knowledge that *anything* could happen at the court of
King Hassan did not seem to help very much, and even a warning from
Princess Margaret—who had visited Morocco in 1976—to expect the
unexpected did not fully prepare the royal party for what lay in store.
On one evening during Princess Margaret's visit, as she, her lady-in-

The Moroccan ruler looks decidedly unimpressed by the Queen's
conversation—perhaps a lecture on the politeness of Kings?

waiting, private secretary and personal detective awaited their official
car to take them off to dinner with the King, Hassan put in a sudden
personal appearance, swept the Princess off to his own two-seater
sports car, drove her round Rabat at high speed regaling her with the
story of his life, and then, just as unceremoniously, deposited her at a
small palace outside the city and bade her goodnight. Diplomatically,
Princess Margaret claimed, though not too convincingly, that she had
thoroughly enjoyed herself.

Four years later the facial expressions—if nothing more—of both
the Queen and Prince Philip told the world of their inner feelings of
anger and indignation at the sudden and frequently inexplicable
disruption, curtailment, cancellation and last-minute alterations to
schedules agreed long beforehand. And each time the offender was the
arrogant King Hassan himself.

Royal tours and all their ramifications are necessarily laid out on
the drawing-board for as long as eighteen months before the Queen is
finally *en route* to her destination. Morocco, however, proved how

easily carefully arranged schedules can disintegrate into confusion and the sovereign herself treated with little more courtesy than the average British tourist.

Perhaps the most symbolic aspect of the Queen's function embraces events which fall beneath the umbrella heading of Royal Ceremonial. These are the grand occasions for which Britain is justly held in such high esteem throughout the world and which no other nation has been able to emulate with nearly the same degree of success or, indeed, brilliance.

The splendid spectacle of Trooping the Colour, or the Sovereign's Birthday Parade as it is otherwise known, springs readily to mind, as does the State Opening of Parliament, the services for the Most Noble Order of the Garter at Windsor, and in Edinburgh, the Order of the Thistle, most ancient of the Scottish orders of chivalry.

Visiting Heads of State—reigning monarchs or incumbent presidents—are received either in London or at Windsor, occasionally in Edinburgh, with the full trappings of pomp and pageantry and, from time to time, royal weddings provide the nation with an intoxicating blend of royal and ecclesiastical magnificence. Less frequent, of course, are the coronations and jubilees of a sovereign. Of the former only four have taken place this century: those of Edward VII and Queen Alexandra in 1902, of George V and Queen Mary in 1911, of George VI and Queen Elizabeth in 1937 and of Elizabeth II herself in 1953. Of the latter there have been only two—the Silver Jubilees of the present Queen's grandfather, King George V, in May 1935 and of Her Majesty in June 1977.

Upon her accession to the throne Elizabeth II succeeded King George VI as Colonel-in-Chief of all the Guards Regiments and the Corps of Royal Engineers, and as Captain-General of the Royal Regiment of Artillery and the Honourable Artillery Company. At her coronation Her Majesty assumed a similar position in relation to a number of other units within the United Kingdom and in other parts of the Commonwealth. Indeed, as sovereign, the Queen is Head of the Army, the Royal Navy and the Royal Air Force, and as such each owes direct allegiance to *her*, not to the state or, in other words, to the government.

It is with the Army that we associate the Queen most readily. The Royal Navy is more in the line of other members of her family. Prince

Philip, for instance, holds the rank of Admiral of the Fleet, Prince Charles—who gave up a naval career in 1976—holds the rank of Commander, Prince Andrew is currently serving as a naval helicopter pilot, and Princess Anne is Chief Commandant of the Women's Royal Naval Service (WRNS).

The ceremony of Trooping the Colour (*never* Trooping *of* the Colour), held each June on Horse Guards Parade to honour the sovereign's birthday, first began in 1755. But at that time it was never the feature of English life it has since become. Until 1958, when the parade was switched to a Saturday, it had nearly always been held on the second Thursday in June—presenting a nightmare of disruption for London's traffic.

Today, the ceremony allows the entire Household Division, which is composed of the Household Cavalry (the Life Guards and the Blues and Royals), and the five regiments of the Guards Division (Grenadier, Coldstream, Scots, Irish and Welsh Guards) to wish the sovereign, their 'Boss', many happy returns.

Two full rehearsals on Horse Guards Parade, in which the Duke of Edinburgh and the Prince of Wales normally participate, precede the actual day of the Trooping, when the Queen, attended by the Princes of the Blood, a host of military personnel and the traditional Sovereign's Escort of the Household Cavalry, sets out from Buckingham Palace to review her troops.

Dressed in the scarlet tunic of the regiment of Guards whose Colour is being trooped, a navy-blue riding skirt, high boots and a bearskin cap reminiscent of a tricorn, to which is affixed the relevant regimental plume, the Queen rides side-saddle as, indeed, she always has since taking part in her first parade when still Princess Elizabeth in 1949. As an equally noble successor to Her Majesty's previous horses, 'Winston', the magnificent chestnut-brown, and 'Doctor' a grey—who was said to have fought and recovered from cancer—the Queen's mount since 1969 has always been 'Burmese', a black Canadian mare, which had been presented to her as a gift.

Nowadays, as the clock on Horse Guards Building sings out its rather flat chime, it is precisely 11 a.m. as the Queen rides on to the parade ground, salutes her mother and takes her appointed place. Some years ago Her Majesty had been very far from pleased to learn that the clock had always been set back or advanced to chime the hour upon her arrival. A subsequent royal command decreed that more time should be allowed for the slowly moving equestrian procession to ride down

the 1,821 yards of the Mall, lined by 428 guardsmen who, like mechanical toy soldiers, snap to attention at the gruffly bellowed order, 'ROYAL SALUTE—*Pre-sent* Arms'.

Once upon a time trooping the 'colour'—the regimental standard—along the ranks was of vital significance. Today it is little more than a symbolic act. In medieval warfare, and even to the battlefield of Inkerman in the Crimea in 1854, men followed their 'colour', which had previously been trooped before them for the purpose of identification. Equally, the Queen's review of the men on parade—although a very real, eagle-eyed, inspection—dates back to the days when the sovereign, in person, led his troops into battle. The last King of England to do so was George II, at the Battle of Dettingen on 27th June 1743.

Contrary to a widely-held belief Trooping the Colour is not a state occasion, unlike, say, the Opening of Parliament. In essence a ritual of the greatest symbolic, even feudal, splendour, the State Opening of Parliament is, perhaps, the most obvious image of royal authority. Having driven from Buckingham Palace in the Irish State Coach, the second most important carriage of the state fleet (the first being the massive State Coach itself), the Queen arrives at the Victoria Tower of the Palace of Westminster and there, preceded by the colourfully-robed Heralds, makes her way to the Royal Robing Room at the top of the Grand Staircase lined by troopers of the Life Guards. There she is arrayed in her crimson Parliamentary robe, puts on the Imperial State Crown, and then processes slowly towards the House of Lords.

Seated upon the Throne the Queen surveys a glittering scene not only representative of the structure of British society as it is today, but as it used to be when the sovereign's power was once absolute. Before her a chamber full of peers and peeresses, a sentence of judges perched, seemingly haphazardly, on a large stuffed 'cushion' known as the Woolsack (normally reserved solely for the Lord Chancellor), a beatitude of bishops on parallel benches and, furthest away, if not quite 'the people' assembled to hear the sovereign's word, then certainly their elected representatives. Led by the Prime Minister, members of the House of Commons are especially summoned from the House 'to attend Her Majesty'. This, after all, is the Queen's Parliament; it is *her* government and, ostensibly, the 'Gracious Speech' delivered from the Throne, is *her* word. In *her* name is justice administered and in *her* name are freedom, law and order upheld and maintained.

Unlike Queen Victoria who, in 1881, refused to approve the 'Gracious Speech' (she was aided and abetted by that wily old fox Disraeli who regarded it as a 'piece of Parliamentary gossip'), Queen Elizabeth II allows that it is the *only* speech to which she will suggest or make no changes whatsoever. Once drawn it will be delivered from the Throne as the incumbent administration desires.

The State Opening of Parliament is probably the shortest of all ceremonial occasions, for once the Queen's duty is done and she has outlined the Government's proposals for the coming year, she retires from the House of Lords to her Robing Room. There she exchanges the Crown for the diamond circlet, or diadem, first made for George IV that she reserves almost exclusively for use on this occasion. The pages-of-honour and ladies-in-waiting unfasten the heavy Parliamentary robe which is then packed away for another year, and Her Majesty slips back into the long, mink-trimmed evening coat of heavily embroidered white satin, originally made for her State Visit to Paris in 1972, and which, like George IV's diadem, she now wears for her progress to and from the Palace of Westminster.

Another of the Queen's titles refers to her as 'The Fount of Honour'. It sounds rather fanciful but does in fact mean that only through the sovereign can honours be bestowed. The majority of awards—with such antiquated, almost meaningless, names as Order or Commander of the British Empire (the OBE and CBE respectively)— are granted at the recommendation of the Prime Minister. It then falls to the Queen, at the fourteen stiffly formal ceremonies of investiture held at Buckingham Palace each year, to bestow some 2,200 decor-ations on worthy recipients. There are certain honours, however, that remain exclusively in the sovereign's personal gift. Included among them are the Order of Merit and the Royal Victorian Order and, of course, at the very top of the English league, the Most Noble Order of the Garter.

History reminds us that this, 'the most noble and amiable company of St George named the Garter', is the most ancient order of 'Christian chivalry' in Britain. With its origins dating back through six centuries, no order could surely have been founded on a more chivalrous or gentlemanly act. Nor, for that matter, is another order ever likely to be established to save a lady's 'honour'. Be that as it may, Joan, Countess of Salisbury, is said to have been responsible for the creation of this distinguished order when, on an April evening in 1349 while dancing with the Plantagenet King, Edward III, she contrived to allow her

blue garter to slip from her thigh. Picking it up off the floor, the King declared to his smirking, winking courtiers, 'Honi soit qui mal y pense' ('Shame on him who thinks evil of it'), which thus became the motto of the Order of the Garter.

Including the Queen, Sovereign of all Orders of Chivalry in Britain, the Garter claims a fixed complement of twenty-six 'Knights'. This number currently includes just three women, save for the Queen herself. They are Queen Elizabeth The Queen Mother, on whom—in one of his first acts as monarch—King George VI bestowed the order on his forty-first birthday in 1936, the present Queen of Denmark, Margrethe II, and the former Queen of the Netherlands, Princess Juliana.

Elizabeth II was herself invested with the Garter (instantly recognizable by its distinctive eight-pointed 'Star' and the broad, blue riband or sash which is always worn over the left shoulder) by her father a few days before her wedding in 1947. Indeed, it is not unreasonable to suppose that the same distinction will be accorded Diana, Princess of Wales, before too long. The Prince of Wales was created a Knight of the Order in 1968.

With or without the installation of new knights, a service for the Order is held, like the Trooping ceremony, each June. When knights are installed, however, the ceremony is conducted in the Throne Room at Windsor Castle. Then, as the Queen buckles a blue and gold garter around the left leg of each recipient in turn, the Prelate, the Bishop of Winchester, proclaims:

'To the honour of God Omnipotent, and in Memorial of the Blessed Martyr, Saint George, tie about thy leg, for thy Renown, this Most Noble Garter. Wear it as the symbol of the Most Illustrious Order never to be forgotten or laid aside, that hereby thou mayest be admonished to be courageous, and having undertaken a just war, into which thou shalt be engaged, thou mayest stand firm, valiantly fight, courageously and successfully conquer.'

After luncheon the full procession forms up and makes its way, on foot, through the upper, middle and lower wards—or precincts—of Windsor Castle to St George's Chapel, the 'Headquarters' of the Order. Watched and applauded by mesmerized crowds who have been admitted on passes issued months before by the Lord Chamberlain, the procession is composed of the elderly but upright, Military

Knights of Windsor, the Heralds in their brilliantly emblazoned tabards and, of course, the Knights. The last but most important figure in this medieval pageant is the Queen herself, invariably dressed in a long white gown, over which is worn the rich, deep blue velvet mantle of the Order, her train borne by two scarlet-coated pages. Completing the picture, Her Majesty wears the white-plumed velvet cap worn by each member of the Order.

While a similar pageant surrounds services held at St Giles' Cathedral in Edinburgh for the Order of the Thistle, the panoply which attends those of less significance is naturally diminished. Nevertheless, when the great doors are opened and St Paul's Cathedral receives the congregation of the 158-year-old Order of St Michael and St George and the Lord Mayor of London, in state dress, greets the Queen robed in blue satin and diamonds, or when the Dean of Westminster welcomes Her Majesty, now attired in a robe of red satin, to Westminster Abbey to honour the Order of the Bath (founded in 1725), even the most cynical observer cannot fail to savour something of the awe-inspiring traditions and magnificence of British Royal Ceremonial. For the Queen, of course, it is all part of the job.

CHAPTER TWO

THE FIRST DECADE

LEFT: The Duke and Duchess of York with the infant Princess Elizabeth
photographed by Marcus Adams in 1927.

The birth of a first child—a daughter—to the Duke and Duchess of York was as much an occasion for public happiness as it was cause for private celebration within the royal family.

At her marriage to Prince Albert, Duke of York, three years earlier, Lady Elizabeth Bowes Lyon had become one of the most popular of royal figures. At twenty-three, as the Duke of Windsor recalled, she 'brought into the family a lively and refreshing spirit', and indeed she had. To all intents and purposes a 'commoner', Elizabeth Lyon was the first of an increasing number of non-royal women who were to marry into the royal family with the passage of time. Already long since passed were the days when any number of acceptable princesses were available to help maintain the purity of the blood royal. As an outsider, Lady Elizabeth had grown up in a happy atmosphere of contentment and freedom, totally unfettered by the kind of bondage that suppressed the majority of her in-laws. Now, as the 'smiling' or 'little' Duchess, she greatly enlivened the image of the monarchy which, if not exactly stolid, had certainly appeared far too remote for far too long.

It was hardly surprising, therefore, that the nation should have taken such pleasure in an announcement made towards the end of 1925 that the Duchess was expecting her first baby.

Without a permanent home of their own in London, however, the Yorks readily accepted the invitation of the Duchess's parents, the Earl and Countess of Strathmore and Kinghorne, to move in to their town residence at 17 Bruton Street, Mayfair, and it was to that tall, aristocratic house that the royal couple travelled from Sandringham in January 1926.

Throughout the next four months a feeling of happy anticipation began to grow—especially as the approximate date of the Duchess's confinement drew near. Then, quite unexpectedly, anxiety clouded the horizon with the discovery that the unborn princess was, in fact, a breech-baby and, on a night of 'evil April drizzle', the royal gynaecologists prepared to deliver the child by Caesarian section.

At Windsor Castle King George V and Queen Mary—the Duke's parents—left instructions when they retired that evening, 20th April, that they must be roused at any hour should news be received from London. At 4 a.m. they were awakened with tidings of the baby's arrival, and later, as the formal announcement was made throughout the Empire proclaiming that 'Her Royal Highness the Duchess of York was safely delivered of a Princess at 2.40 a.m. this morning,

Wednesday, 21st April', Queen Mary addressed her diary, 'Such a relief and joy.'

Twenty-four hours later, the *Morning Post* told its readers,

'All day outside 17 Bruton Street, a crowd stood, oblivious of the heavy showers of rain, waiting—who can say for what? The Duchess of York or the new, tiny Princess they could not have hoped to see; perhaps it was faint expectation of a glimpse of the Duke, or a vague desire to show interest and a fellow-feeling in the royal parents' happiness, that chained them to the pavement.'

Yet despite all the feelings of 'relief and joy', and despite the crowds gathered on the pavement in Bruton Street, the Princess's birth was not regarded as one of any great import. It was, of course, true that she stood third in line to the throne, immediately after her father and his elder brother, Edward, Prince of Wales, and immediately before her uncles Henry and George (later the Dukes of Gloucester and Kent), but it was seen by historians as no more than a temporary situation. What the whole country was still waiting for was the Prince of Wales's marriage and the births of his own children. Then the Duke of York, his daughter, and any further offspring of his line, would be displaced and gradually pushed still further away from the throne.

Sixty years ago such things were of small consideration to the public at large. What mattered most, at least for the time being, was that the popular Duchess of York had given them a new princess and, indeed, had presented the King and Queen with their first granddaughter.

On 29th May the month-old Princess, dressed in the robe of cream satin overlaid with a delicate Honiton lace which had been worn by eight of Queen Victoria's nine children—and nearly every royal baby since—was taken to Buckingham Palace for her christening. There, in the private chapel, before her godparents, three of whom were also her grandparents, King George V, Queen Mary, the Earl of Strathmore, the Princess Mary, the Duke of Connaught and Lady Elphinstone, the Archbishop of Canterbury, Dr Gordon Cosmo Lang, dipped his fingers into water from the River Jordan contained in the golden font, its rim festooned with water-lilies, made the sign of the cross on the baby's forehead and named her Elizabeth Alexandra Mary.

It was clear to all that the first of these names honoured her mother.

The christening of Princess Elizabeth Alexandra Mary of York. Left to right (front row): Lady Elphinstone, Queen Mary, the Duchess of York with the baby Princess, the Countess of Strathmore and Princess Mary. Back row: the Duke of Connaught, King George V, the Duke of York and the Earl of Strathmore.

RIGHT: Princess Elizabeth Alexandra Mary of York—aged one year.

Indeed, it may even have been the Duke of York himself who suggested the idea. For he had not long written to the Queen expressing his great pride in his wife, especially 'after all she has gone through . . .'. The second name was chosen in tribute to George V's mother, Queen Alexandra, who had died only six months earlier, while the last remembered the baby's formidable 'Grannie', Queen Mary herself.

If newspaper coverage of the royal advent had been short-lived, the little Princess was soon to slip from mind altogether as the General Strike hit the nation. Bitterness and discontentment had fermented in Britain since the end of the Great War and widespread strike action seemed the only way of giving forceful voice to the privations, anger and fears of the ordinary men and women who kept the country ticking. Precipitated by the withdrawal of the Government's subsidy to the coal industry and the failure of negotiations over new terms for miners, the industrial north downed tools in response to the strike order set for midnight on 3rd May. Within a fortnight, however, the strike which had paralysed Britain was over and, on 13th May, King George V's rallying call to his people urged them to 'forget whatever elements of bitterness' it may have created, 'and forthwith address ourselves to the task of bringing into being a peace which will be lasting, [one which] looks only to the future with the hopefulness of a united people'.

A year later, when the Duke and Duchess of York were despatched on a six-month antipodean mission, the first time they had officially represented the sovereign abroad, George V and Queen Mary personally took charge of another of Britain's future hopes—their young granddaughter Elizabeth, or 'Lilibet', as she styled herself during her early attempts to pronounce her name. Sending her parents 'the most excellent accounts of your sweet little daughter', the King wrote, 'she has four teeth now which is very good at eleven months old, and she is very happy and drives in a carriage every afternoon, which amuses her'. These daily excursions no doubt played a major part in sowing the seeds of the future Queen's passionate interest in horses; not simply those she saw stabled at the Royal Mews at Buckingham Palace or at Windsor Castle, but those cantering and galloping along Rotten Row, as she was driven round Hyde Park.

As adoring a grandfather as he had been a frequently brusque, insensitive father, George V happily indulged the Princess's fantasies, and on one occasion, the Archbishop of Canterbury, Dr Lang, was

ABOVE: 'She is very happy and drives in a carriage every afternoon ...'
wrote King George V to Princess Elizabeth's parents while they were
touring the Antipodes. The Princess is seen here with her nanny,
'Allah' Knight, leaving No. 145 Piccadilly.

TOP: The Duchess of York with her daughter in 1928.

Princess Elizabeth was presented with her first pony at the age of three.
Here she is seen riding in Windsor Great Park with her father and younger sister
Margaret Rose, April 1939.

astounded to find his sovereign down on all fours, no longer a king but, at that moment, a majestic steed, while Princess Elizabeth—playing the part of a groom—led him across the room by his beard.

At the age of three the fair, curly-headed Princess accompanied the King and Queen to Bognor where 'Grandpapa England' (an apocryphal name legend says 'Lilibet' bestowed on George V) was to recuperate after a serious illness caused by an abscess on a lung. 'She made his convalescence bearable to him', said Mabell, Countess of Airlie, a close friend and a lady-in waiting to Queen Mary.

From birth Princess Elizabeth was placed in the care of an old family friend, the devoted Clara Knight or 'Allah' as she was better known. More than twenty-five years earlier Mrs Knight had been engaged by Lady Strathmore as nanny to her youngest children. She had then moved on to supervise the offspring of Lady Elphinstone, an elder sister of the Duchess of York, and now she found herself employed by 'the little Duchess' herself, in charge of the nursery floor at Number 145 Piccadilly, the Yorks' official residence at Hyde Park Corner which they had finally acquired in 1927. Not nearly so busy a circus as it is today, it was still a far cry from the gracefulness of the Yorks' first home, White Lodge, in Richmond Park, but it was infinitely more convenient for the lives both the Duke and Duchess were obliged to lead.

By 1930, the year in which their second daughter, Princess Margaret, was born, the Duke and Duchess of York had become rather more acclimatized to the ever-increasing interest—from all around the world—that was being shown in the young Princess Elizabeth. At first the Duchess had been almost alarmed by the curious generosity of total strangers who sent her daughter gifts by the sack-load, to say nothing of the volume of letters addressed to 'Princess Betty'. At home as well as abroad, photographs of the Princess adorned the covers of any number of popular magazines, while her outfits set new trends and created a flourishing industry among manufacturers of children's fashions. Almost everywhere mushroomed small 'Lilibet-lookalikes' in dainty dresses, coats and bonnets.

A little later on when she, too, was of an age, the Yorks' younger daughter, Margaret Rose, was invariably dressed in similar style to her sister, something that was to remain quite evident even when both had reached their teens. In due course, Princess Margaret—who had been

born at Glamis Castle, the ancestral seat of the earls of Strathmore, on 21st August 1930—also became an object of mass adulation.

The Duke and Duchess of York were to have no more children, even though it has been said that the Duke, in particular, would have liked a son. There is, however, no reason to believe that he was at all disappointed at having fathered two daughters.

For the York family, happily ensconced at 145 Piccadilly, a four-storeyed house containing some thirty rooms, where a Household staff of twenty— from a butler to an odd-job man—was employed, life tended to follow a comfortable, well-ordered routine. As active participants in what was later to be called the 'royal road show', the Duke and Duchess were careful to guard the cherished privacy of their home life—that all important safety valve in the existence of very public figures. In 1931 there were made two—and each in its own way, enriching—additions to their lives. First the King had given them a country estate of their own, the Royal Lodge in Windsor Great Park. The house itself, though not especially outstanding from an architectural point of view, was still a handsome, even imposing, structure which soon won its new occupants' deepest and abiding affection. Washed a sugar-icing pink, it stands well secluded from prying eyes, surrounded by immaculate grounds, originally the result of the Duke of York's own strenuous labours. From a veritable jungle, he had created an extensive and appealing garden of avenues and glades, brought to life by banks of brilliantly-coloured rhododendron and azalea bushes. Here the family would spend a good deal of their leisure time throughout the year.

The second addition was Miss Marion Crawford, a young Scotswoman who had been engaged by the Duke and Duchess to act as governess to their daughters. Princess Elizabeth's nick-name for this slender woman from Dunfermline was 'Crawfie', and by that diminutive she was invariably known to the end of her career in royal service almost twenty years later. Though competent and agreeable, the twenty-two-year-old Miss Crawford did not meet unconditional approval. Queen Mary considered her far too young, while Allah Knight waged something of a cold war against her in retaliation for laying claim to her elder charge. This resentment at losing control was one of the reasons why Allah, the archetypal British nanny, kept Princess Margaret in the nursery—and therefore to herself—for as long as she reasonably could.

For her royal pupils Crawfie devised a comprehensive time-table of

lessons which followed much the same lines as those found in any good private school. The week always began with half an hour's religious instruction every Monday morning, otherwise arithmetic occupied the time allowed for the first lesson. Then followed instruction in history, grammar, geography, literature and writing. (One of the King's few direct charges to the governess had been 'For God's sake teach Lilibet and Margaret a decent hand!') Madame Montaudon-Smith, 'Monty', gave them French lessons and during the holidays Mlle Georgina Guérin was at hand to keep their French conversation up to scratch. There were swimming, and later, life-saving, lessons; Miss Betty Vacani taught dancing; singing classes were held at the nearby home of Lady Cavan, while the rest of the Princesses' curriculum was taken up with drawing and music lessons and the still more pleasurable riding instruction at Royal Lodge, under the tutelage of Mr Owen, the groom. At Queen Mary's suggestion, her granddaughters were occasionally taken on museum outings or to view an art collection, and on one well-known occasion they travelled, more or less incognito, by tube train to Tottenham Court Road, took tea at the YWCA, were eventually recognized and, as a crowd gathered around them, had to be rescued by a hastily summoned royal car.

The problem then, and it is almost as true today, was that the public was so unaccustomed to seeing members of the royal family out and about like themselves that, once spotted, they could never escape the lingering, though well meant, attention of strangers. It was, in fact, a problem both Princess Elizabeth and her sister already knew well from their playtime activities in Hamilton Gardens, at the back of 145 Piccadilly. For there, as they threw themselves into their games, faces always gathered at the open railings to watch. It was, said Princess Margaret much later in life, something she and her sister never got used to.

By and large, of course, the Princesses' childhood was spent in the company of adults. And although they often enjoyed visits to their younger Bowes Lyon cousins, especially to the Elphinstones, and later befriended the girls from within court circles who joined the Buckingham Palace patrols of Girl Guides and Brownies, to which the Princesses naturally belonged, they were never allowed to mix freely with their contemporaries. The result, according to Crawfie, was that other children held 'an enormous fascination, like mystic beings from another world'.

In those days there was no question about the way in which the

ABOVE: Seated between her grandmother Queen Mary and her aunt the Princess Royal, 'Lilibet' drives with her mother to Trooping the Colour.

LEFT: The young Princess in the role of train-bearer to her kinswoman, Lady May Cambridge, daughter of Princess Alice and the Earl of Athlone, 1931.

Princesses were to be raised. The idea of being sent off to proper schools, thus mingling with other children, was never seriously considered by their parents and, in any event, King George V with his reactionary attitudes would never have permitted it. A decade later— and in another reign—the Princesses' cousins, Prince Edward, Duke of Kent, and Princess Alexandra, did go off to school and not long afterwards they were followed by the Duke of Gloucester's sons, William and Richard.

Yet despite their relatively isolated positions, the Princesses Elizabeth and Margaret appeared not to have hankered after other forms of companionship and ultimately emerged from adolescence as well-adjusted, albeit somewhat shy, young women.

If Princess Elizabeth's early years had taught her that she would always be a focus of intense interest in her own right, they were also to introduce her to the kind of occasions which, on a much broader scale, tended to arouse considerable public attention. Her first lesson came at the age of five when she took part in her first 'society' wedding. The bride, Lady May Cambridge, born Princess May of Teck, was the only daughter of the King's cousin Princess Alice, Countess of Athlone, and Queen Mary's brother 'Alge', the Earl of Athlone. It was at Lady May's wedding to Captain (now Sir) Henry Abel Smith, at a village church in Sussex in October 1931, that Princess Elizabeth acted as a train-bearer. Among the adult bridesmaids, it is of interest to note, were the future Queen Ingrid of Denmark, Princess Sibylla of Coburg who, as Crown Princess of Sweden, would become the mother of the present Swedish King, and a young woman who, only four years later, would marry Prince Henry, Duke of Gloucester. She was the Lady Alice Montagu Douglas Scott, at whose wedding both the Princesses Elizabeth and Margaret would act as bridesmaids.

The first full scale *royal* occasion in which the young Princess Elizabeth took an active part, however, was at the wedding of her uncle 'Georgie', the Duke of Kent, to the lovely Princess Marina of Greece and Denmark. Married at Westminster Abbey in November 1934, the bridal couple were a dazzlingly attractive pair on the social scene; a couple who were equally as popular as the Duke and Duchess of York and perhaps, at that time, even more so.

George of Kent, the fourth son of King George V, was a handsome young man of strong artistic inclination. Next to his elder brother the

The Princess acts as bridesmaid at the wedding of Prince George,
Duke of Kent and Princess Marina of Greece and Denmark,
November 1934.

King George V and Queen Mary during one
of the Silver Jubilee drives, 1935.

The Silver Jubilee of King George V and Queen Mary, May 1935.
The royal family in prayer behind their Majesties during the
thanksgiving service at St Paul's Cathedral.

Prince of Wales, Prince George was the most charismatic and cultured of the royal princes. Princess Marina, who emerged from Parisian exile to become his bride, was no less charismatic, immediately establishing an affectionate rapport with the nation. The youngest of the three daughters of Prince and Princess Nicholas of Greece, she was a highly intelligent, sophisticated young woman of Russian, Danish and Greek extract, who brought enormous style and elegance to the British royal house, just as—more than forty years later—the Czech-born Baroness Marie Christine von Reibnitz was to do when she married Prince Michael of Kent in 1978.

Prince George and Princess Marina's wedding on the morning of 29th November 1934 provided a spectacle which held the crowds spellbound. It was the first occasion of its kind since the Duke and Duchess of York had been married at Westminster Abbey eleven years earlier, and the response to it was one of overwhelming delight. The Prince of Wales acted as his brother's best man, and among the bridesmaids, no fewer than five of whom were Princesses, the youngest, aged ten, was the fair-haired Princess Elizabeth of York. Wearing a short dress of white tulle and a bandeau of white roses in her hair, she and the Marquess of Cambridge's young daughter Mary, who would one day act as a bridesmaid to Princess Elizabeth herself, walked in procession immediately after the bride, attired in white and silver brocade, the diamond fringe tiara that was the wedding gift of the City of London securing her long and voluminous veil of white tulle.

The following May a far grander and still more significant occasion was observed throughout the Empire: the Silver Jubilee of King George V's reign. As was to happen forty-two years later, when the twenty-fifth anniversary of Elizabeth II's accession was celebrated, a formal service of thanksgiving was held at St Paul's Cathedral amid splendid scenes of pomp and pageantry. On that day, 6th May 1935, two future Queens (Princess Elizabeth and her mother) rode to the Cathedral together in one of the semi-state landaus, acknowledging the greetings of the exultant crowds thronging the City streets.

Seated opposite the Duke and Duchess of York, Princess Elizabeth and her sister were described by 'Chips' (Sir Henry) Channon, as 'two tiny pink children', while one contemporary newspaper report exclaimed, 'The Princesses captured the hearts of the multitude instantly. The dignified self-possession of Princess Elizabeth and the laughing happiness of her little sister sent the crowds into raptures.

While the children waved their hands with an entire lack of self-consciousness the crowd roared with delight.'

The last of the old-school monarchs—son of King Edward VII and grandson of Queen Victoria—George V embodied most people's idea of kingly dignity. Indeed, he and his consort Queen Mary projected an awesomely majestic image which almost placed them—and quite deliberately so—on a par with the gods.

As King, George V was vehemently opposed to 'daylight' penetrating the mystical shadows of the monarchy. 'If you bring it down to the people, it will lose its mystery and influence', argued one of the King's strongest allies, his Keeper of the Privy Purse, Sir Frederick Ponsonby. Yet 'the people' *wanted* to see more clearly and, consequently, a number of hilariously insignificant tit-bits, contained in 'The Intimate Revelations of a A Royal Photographer', published in a souvenir edition of the popular tabloid the *Daily Mirror*, found a ready and avaricious audience.

'I have seen various beverages mentioned in the Press as the favourite drink of the King, varying from tea and coffee to whisky and port wine', the anonymous author began. 'They are all wrong. Actually His Majesty has a great liking for cocoa. It is by far his favourite drink.' A little further on, readers were treated to 'two other interesting little facts about the King which only his very close friends know. His Majesty's arms are tatooed and he has a lady chiropodist'.

Later still it was revealed that Queen Mary 'always used to darn her stockings herself. I mean, of course, for small repairs. If they were badly worn she had a new pair, but I have often seen her busy with her needle on a small ladder or hole.'

It isn't very likely that such intimate 'revelations' made the Jubilee crowds cheer any more forcefully, but such innocuous glimpses into 'royal life' as these helped to make the King and Queen seem a little more human and, as much then as now, inside stories were devoured with relish by a worshipping public.

Of the Jubilee celebration itself, Fleet Street could hardly have been more descriptive:

'From the sunlit streets into the sunlit Cathedral came faint echoes of cheering—men and women of England paying homage to their King and Queen. In St Paul's there was silence as the great congregation awaited their Majesties. Up Ludgate Hill the cheering grew till it filled the nave, and then burst into a roar as the King and Queen entered the west door.

Between hundreds of beautifully-dressed women and men in shining uniforms the King and Queen walked to the red thrones before the altar.

Behind them came the Royal Family. Women craned forward to see what thy would wear: Queen Mary dressed from head to foot in silver, a huge collar of white fox-fur about her shoulders, a silver aigrette clipped to her hat; the Duchess of York in blue trimmed with grey fur to offset the colour. Beside her bobbed the pink bonnets of the two little Princesses Elizabeth and Margaret Rose. Then the Duchess of Kent. She wore an enormous brimmed hat of an odd shade—something between cream and fawn—a shade which looked calm in that sea of turbulent colour.

"For all that our King has meant to us and has given to us, and for the way by which, during these twenty-five years, this people has been led, it behoves us to offer our thanksgiving to Almighty God". With these words, the Archbishop of Canterbury echoed the thoughts of the Empire in his address at the Jubilee service . . .'

The royal party preparing to leave St Paul's Cathedral after the Silver Jubilee service 1935. The Duke and Duchess of York with their daughters are followed by the Duke and Duchess of Kent.

Amid all the glowing descriptions of the day's events in London, enterprising journalists looked further afield and one in particular came up with an aborigine's testament of faith in his sovereign. Part of the story ran:

> 'In Central Australia lives, in the bush, Charley Cooper, aboriginal. He has never seen the King; probably never will. The King means this to him . . .
>
> "I been know about the King of England. That's our Boss. Him been save us in this country. When white man come along all this stealing business first been startim, and shoot a few of our people, the boss up at the telegraph station stoppem from not kill us blackfellow. The King been give us rations; give us place . . . Boss told me all about not to be frightened. . . . He told me you fellows gottem white-fellow King. . . . He told me he's got gold top on his head. He used to tell me you needn't be frightened, he look after you people. I think this King, he good for us." '

Within the year jubilation across the Empire had turned to sorrow, for the King with the 'gold top on his head' was dead.

George V's death at Sandringham on 20th January 1936 raised the curtain on a drama that was to last eleven months, culminating in the abdication of the new King—Edward VIII or 'David', as he was known to his family— and the accession of his younger brother 'Bertie', the Duke of York, as King George VI.

As Prince of Wales, Edward VIII had developed a very singular taste for married women. Some said he looked less for a lover than a mother, while others flippantly remarked that his affairs with women who made cuckolds of their husbands lessened the chances of paternity suits landing at the Prince's door.

Throughout 1936, however, infinitely more was at stake. In the autumn of 1931, at a house party in Melton Mowbray, the Prince had met the American-born Wallis Simpson. Handsome, rather than beautiful, Mrs Simpson possessed a refreshingly direct manner which, coupled with an agreeably extrovert personality, enchanted the Prince—especially after all the twittering, empty-headed debutantes he invariably encountered. Throughout the next four years friendship blossomed into love and what, at first, had tended to be regarded—by those in the know—as a relatively harmless liaison, rapidly assumed the guise of a grave constitutional issue.

When at last the story of 'the King and Mrs Simpson' became general knowledge, public debate divided the nation into two camps—those who wanted to see Edward VIII remain on the throne and those who, in the circumstances, did not. At the end of the day the King lost his battle against 'the Establishment' and, accordingly, relinquished his crown. His last act as sovereign was to sign the Instrument of Abdication. This he did at Fort Belvedere, his beloved country home in Windsor Great Park, on the morning of 10th December 1936.

It is just possible to picture the scene at Number 145 Piccadilly that day, as a somewhat bemused, but excited, Princess Elizabeth told her sister, 'Uncle David is going away and isn't coming back, and Papa is to be King'. Although only six years old, Princess Margaret also managed to grasp the implications of her sister's news and, with eyes widening in amazement, her thoughts racing ahead into the future, she asked, 'Does that mean you are going to be *Queen*?'

Though we know that George VI's reaction to his brother's abdication was one of shocked disbelief, which in turn led to a nervous breakdown, it is impossible to imagine, much less fully appreciate, the maelstrom of emotions that assailed him at that time. Ever since childhood he had lacked confidence in himself, and a strong sense of inferiority had been compounded still further by the speech impediment he had endeavoured to overcome as a young man.

Since their marriage it had fallen to the Duchess of York, now Queen Elizabeth, to support and encourage her husband to an extraordinary degree. This she had managed with very considerable success, but now she needed every last ounce of courage and fortitude to help her in a task that had never weighed more heavily on her shoulders.

With their own world turned upside down, the new King and Queen were anxious that their daughters' lives should not be disrupted more than was absolutely necessary; and to all intents and purposes, the Princesses took their sudden elevation very much in their stride.

Early in the new year, 1937, King George and Queen Elizabeth took up residence at Buckingham Palace, and were joined there in the middle of February by their daughters. From then until May all was a hive of activity in preparation for their Majesties' coronation. A year before, 12th May had been reserved for the ritual enthronement of the exiled Prince on whom, that March, the King had conferred the title, Duke of Windsor.

ABOVE: King George VI and Queen Elizabeth with their daughters acknowledge the crowds' cheers from the balcony of Buckingham Palace.

ABOVE RIGHT: Coronation Day, 1937. Princess Margaret wearily rests her head on the edge of the royal gallery, under the watchful eye of her grandmother. 'She is very young for a coronation, isn't she?' Princess Elizabeth had asked.

RIGHT: Marcus Adams's romantic portrait of the Princesses Elizabeth and Margaret.

The coronation of their parents was to prove a long but exhilarating day for the Princesses, one which entailed scenes of high solemnity, rich symbolic significance, magnificent theatre and carnival-like jubilation. Princess Elizabeth had just passed her eleventh bithday; Princess Margaret was not yet seven.

Was it an occasion, wondered the elder Princess, that her sister could take comfortably in her stride? Concerned that it might be something of a tiresome ordeal, Princess Elizabeth asked, 'She is very young for a coronation, isn't she?' The answer was very probably 'yes', but tiresome ordeals and long-winded ceremonies are a part of the royal family's public life, and an early experience of one of the longest royal rituals imaginable could only stand the young Princess Margaret—indeed would stand *both* Princesses—in good stead for later tests of royal endurance.

For the coronation the Princesses were to wear identical dresses of white lace, adorned with small silver bows, while from their shoulders

would fall trains of purple velvet trimmed with ermine. At the King's request, lightweight coronets were also fashioned for his daughters. On the day itself the Princesses set out from Buckingham Palace in the Irish State Coach, accompanied by their aunt Mary, the Princess Royal, and her son George, Viscount Lascelles (now the Earl of Harewood). Upon their arrival at Westminster Abbey, they made their way through the Royal Entrance and into the nave. There, preceded by Rouge Croix Pursuivant and Rouge Dragon Pursuivant and two gentleman ushers, Princess Elizabeth and her sister led the procession of British royalties towards the Royal Gallery, looking out across the Coronation Theatre from above the tomb of Anne of Cleves.

When at last the lengthy ceremony finally came to an end, and the King and Queen had each been anointed, invested with the regalia and enthroned, the young Princesses returned to Buckingham Palace, this time driving in state with their grandmother Queen Mary, and their great-aunt Maud, the Queen of Norway.

That evening the King wrote at length about the day's events, recording every detail in the diary he faithfully kept. His mother, too, noted some of her thoughts. Queen Mary wrote, 'I sat between Maud & Lilibet, & Margaret came next. They looked too sweet in their lace dresses & robes, especially when they put on their coronets. Bertie & E. looked so well when they came in & did it all too beautifully. The service was wonderful & impressive—we were all much moved . . . a wonderful day!'

Princess Elizabeth also made a record of her impressions in an essay dedicated to her parents and headed, 'The Coronation, 12th May 1937'. Preserved in the Royal Library at Windsor Castle among the jealously guarded collection of private documents to which no author has yet been granted access, the Heiress Presumptive (as the Princess now was) described every gripping detail, from the moment she first leapt out of bed and 'crouched in the window looking on to a cold, misty morning', to the exhausted moment—some fourteen hours later—when her day finally drew to a close.

LEFT: **Her Royal Highness The Heiress Presumptive.**

CHAPTER THREE

PATHWAY TO THE THRONE

LEFT: During the Second World War, the Princesses were said by the Censor to be 'living somewhere in England'. That 'somewhere' was Windsor Castle. Against a formal setting Princess Elizabeth and her sister pose for Marcus Adams.

As the menacing shadow of Nazi Germany spread across Europe during the late 1930s, so hopes of continued world peace diminished. In an increasingly tense political atmosphere King George VI and Queen Elizabeth undertook two State Visits abroad: to Paris in July 1938 and to the United States the following May.

Both visits were resoundingly successful, not only enhancing the popularity of the King and Queen, but re-affirming bonds of friendship between allies. Neither visit could have been better timed,

The royal family riding in the Home Park at Windsor.

for less than three months after their Majesties' return from North America, Britain was at war with Germany for the second time in little more than twenty years.

It was at the start of the royal family's summer holiday at Balmoral in 1939 that the Second World War was declared, and while they returned to London with all speed and urgency, the King and Queen decided it would be best for their daughters to stay on in Scotland. There the Princesses remained, in fact, until December when, to their intense joy, they learned that Christmas would be spent at Sandringham as usual, and were taken into Aberdeen to buy small trinkets to give to their parents as gifts. For the most part, however, the Princesses Elizabeth and Margaret Rose spent the war living quietly 'somewhere in England'. It didn't need the mind of a genius to work out that that 'somewhere' was, of course, Windsor Castle, in the county of Berkshire, not more than twenty miles from London.

There, while the Luftwaffe passed overhead, they spent their nights in what Princess Margaret has described as 'a concrete box',

The royal family at Dartmouth in 1939. Behind them Lord Mountbatten and his nephew Prince Philip of Greece (in white topped cap) laugh at something they have just heard.

constructed beneath one of the private royal towers. Otherwise, their days still followed the familiar routine pattern of study and recreation, under Crawfie's watchful eye. Even the Buckingham Palace Girl Guide troop followed them to Windsor so that, in so far as was possible, 'normality' was observed in the abnormal climate of wartime Britain. Christmas provided a variation on a well-known theme with the

Christmas pantomimes at Windsor Castle. ABOVE: *Aladdin*, 1943, and RIGHT: *Old Mother Red Riding Boots*, 1944.

Princesses' participation in the now famous pantomimes, staged in the vast Waterloo Chamber before specially invited audiences. The first, put on in 1941, was *Cinderella*, followed in subsequent years by *The Sleeping Beauty*, *Aladdin* and *Old Mother Red Riding Boots*.

Pantomimes were not the only form of entertainment, however, and indeed, several other shows and concerts were staged at Windsor

in aid of various charities involved in war work. During one such 'gala' evening hosted by the King and Queen, this time to assist the British Red Cross, Princess Elizabeth appeared as a solo artiste and, to the sound of a lone violin, danced a French Minuet as well as a Scottish reel.

During those 'missing' years in the lives of the generation of which the King's daughters were a part, Princess Elizabeth matured into womanhood. In 1942 at the age of sixteen, George VI created her Colonel of the Grenadier Guards and, two years later, while King George was touring battlefields in Italy, she was appointed a Counsellor of State for the first time.

As she grew up Princess Elizabeth became increasingly eager to do something more positive with her time and her abundant energy. Christmas pantomimes, 'digging for victory', an occasional public function and so on seemed all very good, but like so many young people she was anxious to play her part in the war effort and had constantly agitated to be allowed to join up. Early in 1945 her wish was finally granted and, as No. 230873 Second Subaltern HRH The Princess Elizabeth of the Auxiliary Territorial Service, Transport Division, she reported for training. She learned how to strip and service an engine, became proficient in vehicle maintenance, was 'reviewed' by the King and Queen, and again by the Princess Royal—which, as she told her father, opened her eyes to all the fuss a royal visit created—but was never actually called to 'active service'. Nevertheless by the war's end, the Princess had proven her abilities and had been promoted, on merit, to the rank of Junior Commander.

Throughout the years 1939 to 1945 the royal family shared with their subjects the privations of war; they experienced the partial destruction of their home at Buckingham Palace, they knew anxiety over relations held prisoner, and they grieved at the loss of the King's brother, George, Duke of Kent, who died in an aircrash while on active service with the RAF in August 1942.

Though it seems never to have bothered them unduly, the King and Queen also lived with the ever-present threat of assassination by the enemy. Other monarchs such as Haakon, King of Norway, and Wilhelmina, Queen of the Netherlands, took to their heels and fled their countries, sending messages of hope and encouragement to their peoples from the relative safety of Britain or Canada. Conversely,

Training with the ATS; Second Subaltern Elizabeth Windsor, No. 230873.

A wartime engagement. The Queen with Princess Elizabeth in 1944.

King George and Queen Elizabeth knew that their place was with their subjects and resolutely stayed put. 'I shan't go down like the others!' the Queen declared when learning to use a revolver.

Almost six years after it began, the Second World War ended and victory in Europe, V-E Day, brought jubilant masses onto the streets and, in particular, flocking to Buckingham Palace to cheer their sovereigns. Joining the King and Queen on the palace balcony were their daughters: the King impeccable in naval uniform and Princess Elizabeth dressed in the Khaki of the ATS. That day the royal family, or 'We Four' as George VI often referred to Queen Elizabeth, the Princesses and himself, made several appearances in response to the crowd's united cry, 'We want the King'.

Forty years later Elizabeth II recalled V-E Day. In a rare and exclusive interview, recorded for BBC Radio, Her Majesty told Godfrey Talbot:

'I think we went to the balcony nearly every hour, six times, and when the excitement of the floodlights being switched on got through to us my sister and I realized we couldn't see what the crowds were enjoying.

'My mother had put her tiara on for the occasion, so we asked my parents if we could go out and see for ourselves. I remember we were terrified of being recognized, so I pulled my uniform cap well down over my eyes. A Grenadier officer amongst our party of about sixteen people said he refused to be seen in the company of another officer improperly dressed, so I had to put my cap on normally.

'We cheered the King and Queen on the balcony and then walked miles through the streets. I remember lines of unknown people linking arms and walking down Whitehall, all of us just swept along on a tide of happiness and relief.'

At about this time Princess Elizabeth found herself being swept along on a rather less fleeting tide of happiness, one called love. Though they had, of course, met several times before, the Princess's first 'official', or at least, public, meeting with her third cousin, Prince Philip of Greece and Denmark, took place at the Royal Naval College, Dartmouth, shortly before the outbreak of war. The King, himself one of the college's most distinguished 'old boys', wished to see how the cadets were shaping up at that critical moment, and on 22nd July 1939, accompanied by the Queen, the two Princesses and Lord Mount-

batten, he sailed into Dartmouth harbour aboard the then royal yacht *Victoria and Albert*, at the start of a two-day formal visit.

Deputed to entertain Princess Elizabeth and her sister was the eighteen-year-old Prince Philip, already an outstanding Cadet Captain and the holder of the much coveted King's Dirk. He was tall, slim, blond and handsome with 'very bright blue eyes' and, according to his cousin, Princess Marina, Duchess of Kent, had 'inherited the good looks of both sides of the family'. 'He seems intelligent too', the Princess added. 'I should say he has plenty of common sense.' At eighteen he was also strong-willed and bumptious, and a 'cool' streak in his character led some to detect a touch of arrogance and thoughtlessness.

That encounter between Princess Elizabeth and Prince Philip at Dartmouth was recalled many years later by Marion Crawford in her first book *The Little Princesses*. In it 'Crawfie' claimed that her charge 'never took her eyes off [Philip] the whole time. At the tennis courts I thought he showed off a good deal, but the little girls were much impressed. Lilibet said, "How good he is Crawfie! How high he can jump".' Miss Crawford's recollections of the Princesses, though lively and colourful, are not entirely free of embellishment and, although often quoted, are not entirely accurate as, indeed, Princess Margaret once advised the present author. One whose prose was less fanciful was Queen Alexandra of Yugoslavia. In her memoirs she recalled a conversation between the Queen and Prince Philip, in which they looked back at their meeting at the Royal Naval College. 'You were so shy,' the Prince reminded the Queen; 'I couldn't get a word out of you.'

If, as we are led to believe, Princess Elizabeth was smitten by her cousin at the age of only thirteen, Prince Philip took little notice, and not surprisingly. Youths of eighteen are not generally given to thoughts of marriage and they certainly were not at a time when girls of the Princess's age were still regarded very much as children.

At all events the day came when Prince Philip began to take a deeper and more affectionate interest in England's future Queen and, as she grew into young adulthood, that interest led to romance. So it was that throughout 1946 a regular flow of 'Philip says . . . ' or 'Philip thinks . . .', Philip this and Philip that, punctuated Princess Elizabeth's every conversation, leaving the King and Queen—and, of course, the sister in whom she confided—in no doubt that she had found the man of her dreams. Yet while George VI very much approved of Prince

LEFT: **The Princesses at Windsor.**

ABOVE: **Prince Philip of Greece and Denmark accompanies his future in-laws
to the wedding of Lord Mountbatten's daughter Patricia,
in October 1946.**

Philip, not least because he had served the Navy with distinction and had been mentioned in despatches during the Battle of Cape Matapan, the King was only too well aware that his daughter had readily given her heart to the first man to have aroused her emotions. At Windsor she and Princess Margaret had had little opportunity to socialize with Britain's younger grandees and, apart from the more elderly members of their parents' households, had had relatively little contact with the opposite sex.

In any event—as he told Queen Mary—the King considered 'Lilibet' too young for marriage and was determined that she and Philip should bide their time. In the interim, George VI and Queen Elizabeth were accompanied by the Princesses when they undertook a major tour of South Africa at the start of 1947. Not only was this the royal family's first post-war visit overseas, but for Princess Elizabeth and her sister, the one which marked their debut on the ambassadorial carousel. For the King it was also to prove his last tour of duty. The royal family set sail from Portsmouth aboard HMS *Vanguard* on 1st February. Before them lay a strenuous schedule that would take them on a momentous 23,000 mile progress.

From wherever they stopped, be it at official ports of call or when the royal train closed down for the night, Princess Elizabeth was in almost constant touch with Prince Philip by way of telephone and letter. Yet all the same, the tour seemed to last for an eternity and, indeed, many who saw her thought the Princess looked grave and even miserable when compared to the glowing vivacity of Princess Margaret and the serene performances of Queen Elizabeth. While in South Africa, Princess Elizabeth came of age and redeemed herself in the eyes of the disappointed when, from Cape Town, on her twenty-first birthday, she broadcast to the peoples of the empire. It was no ordinary broadcast, but one of dutiful dedication. In part she said, 'I declare before you that my whole life, whether it be long or short, shall be devoted to your service and the service of our great Imperial Commonwealth to which we all belong. But I shall not have strength to carry out this resolution unless you join in it with me, as I now invite you to do. I know that your support will be unfailingly given. God bless all of you who are willing to share it.'

In London during the royal family's absence, a notice appeared in the *London Gazette* on 18th March to the effect that HRH Prince Philip of

Greece and Denmark had become plain Lieutenant Philip Mountbatten, RN, a naturalized British subject. To most it was no more than a formality required of any foreigner who wished to pursue a career in the armed forces. To 'Chips' Channon, Member of Parliament and collector of VIPs, it was a sign that the former Prince was finally approaching the starting gate to a new career as royal consort.

On 21st January 1941, while staying at the British Legation in Athens, Channon had attended 'an enjoyable Greek cocktail party'. 'Philip of Greece was there', he noted in his diary. 'He is extraordinarily handsome, and I recalled my afternoon's conversation with Princess Nicholas [mother of Princess Marina, Duchess of Kent]. He is to be our Prince Consort, and that is why he is serving in our Navy. He is charming, but I deplore such a marriage; he and Princess Elizabeth are too inter-related.' There were many at home who would also 'deplore' the marriage, but on the grounds of Philip's foreign origins, not because he and George VI's daughter shared much the same blood line.

Was there, however, in Channon's mention of a conversation with Princess Nicholas of Greece, a hint of a masterly and carefully concealed plan for a merging of dynasties? Or was it simply that Channon had been quick to read between the hopeful lines of Princess Nicholas's references to her nephew? No matter what, King George VI finally gave his blessing to Princess Elizabeth's engagement and, on 10th July 1947, it was 'with the greatest pleasure' that Their Majesties announced 'the betrothal of their dearly beloved daughter . . .'.

That evening, as cheering crowds pressed against the railings of Buckingham Palace, the Princess and her fiancé, she dressed in a long, V-neck, silk dress and jacket, he in evening suit, a carnation in his lapel, made an impromptu balcony appearance, and the following day press photographers were admitted to snap the happy couple, strolling arm in arm across the terrace, forming a group with the King, the Queen and Princess Margaret in the White Drawing Room, and on their own again with the Princess sitting in an ornate armchair, smiling up at her husband-to-be, uncomfortably balanced on one of the gilded arms.

The morning press welcomed the news from Buckingham Palace with warm, congratulatory articles, and the *Daily Express*, in what was almost a parody of Walter Bagehot, told its readers that 'The announcement of the betrothal of Princess Elizabeth and Lieutenant Mountbatten heightens the ordinary man's sense of history. It enables

A formal engagement study of
Princess Elizabeth and Lieutenant Philip Mountbatten, RN.

him to project the past into the future and to see the rich pattern of events.'

Four months later the marriage of Princess Elizabeth, although officially described as an 'austerity wedding', added one more rich event to the annals of royal history and afforded the nation a day of glittering ceremonial, last seen a full decade earlier at the coronation of the King and Queen.

On the morning of Thursday, 20th November, a Sovereign's Escort of the Household Cavalry assembled in the forecourt of Buckingham Palace, waiting to ride down the Mall accompanying the bride and her father to Westminster Abbey. Kitted out, by order of His Majesty, in full dress uniforms, the 126 troopers waited in the rain for the emergence of the Irish State Coach from the Inner Quadrangle, unaware that inside the palace two last minute panics had sent up a hue and cry. First, the band of the bride's tiara, loaned by her mother, had snapped just as it was being put on to her head; then the bridal bouquet of white orchids could not be located. A jeweller, summoned with the speed of light, made a temporary repair to the diamond tiara and, though it looked slightly askew, the bride put it on. Moments later, a triumphant footman appeared with the missing flowers which had been discovered in a refrigerator where somebody had put them to keep the blooms fresh. After that all was perfection.

Princess Elizabeth, resplendent in Norman Hartnell's Botticelli-inspired gown of ivory duchess satin, embroidered with stars and wheat, garlands of York roses and orange blossom, all worked in crystal and raised seed pearls, her silk veil falling in three separate panels from her hastily repaired headdress, climbed into the the carriage and, to the cheers of crowds more than twenty deep in places along the processional route, set off to join her bridegroom who only the night before had become His Royal Highness The Duke of Edinburgh. (Yet while George VI had elevated Lieutenant Mountbatten to royal status once more, he was not to become a 'prince' again until so created by the Queen in 1957.)

At the west door of the abbey the royal bride was greeted by her eight bridesmaids, Princess Margaret, Princess Alexandra of Kent, Lady Caroline Montagu Douglas Scott, Lady Mary Cambridge, Lady Elizabeth Lambart, the Honourable Margaret Elphinstone, Miss Diana Bowes Lyon and the Honourable Pamela Mountbatten. Her

LEFT, ABOVE: Princess Elizabeth and The Duke of Edinburgh kneel before the high altar in Westminster Abbey during their wedding service. Prince William of Gloucester and Prince Michael of Kent carry the bride's train while Princess Margaret, as chief bridesmaid holds the bride's bouquet of white orchids.

LEFT, BELOW: The Royal Wedding, 1947.

two page-boys, the Princes William of Gloucester and Michael of Kent, picked up her long train and, as a fanfare sounded by twelve trumpeters of the Royal Military School of Music faded away, the King led his daughter along the nave to the sound of the choir singing the hymn, 'Praise, My Soul, the King of Heaven'.

It had been Princess Elizabeth's own wish that the actual solemnization of the marriage should be taken from the Book of Common Prayer, including the vow to 'obey' and, as a compliment to her parents, that the rest of the service should follow the lines observed at their own wedding, nearly twenty-five years earlier. During the opening part of the ceremony the King remained by his daughter's side as the Dean of Westminster reminded bride and groom that matrimony was a Holy Estate 'not by any to be enterprised, nor taken in hand unadvisedly, lightly or wantonly . . .'. Later on the Archbishop of York told the bridal couple:

'Never before has a wedding been followed with such intense interest by so many. . . . One of you, the daughter of our much-loved King and Queen, has gained already by charm and simple grace the affection of all; and the other, as a sailor, has a sure place in the hearts of a people who know how much they owe to the strong shield of the Royal Navy.

'Notwithstanding the splendour and national significance of the service in this Abbey, it is in all essentials the same as it would be for any cottager who might be married this afternoon in some small country church in a remote village in the Dales. The same vows are taken; the same prayers are offered, and the same blessings are given. Everywhere and always this service is built round the taking of vows and the receiving of a blessing . . .

'So with high and confident hope for all that this day means for yourselves and the nation, we send you forth from the Abbey to the great multitudes outside who are eagerly waiting to welcome you as man and wife. You go forth with the affectionate good wishes of all who are here. May God's unfailing love always surround and protect you. May He day by day give you in your married life every blessing, peace and happiness.'

From the Abbey the bride, now officially known as Princess Elizabeth, Duchess of Edinburgh, and her husband travelled back to Buckingham Palace, as tradition decrees, in the Glass Coach. They were followed in turn by the King and Queen Elizabeth, Queen Mary and Princess Andrew of Greece—Prince Philip's widowed mother, with whom the bride was to establish an especially close and happy relationship in the years ahead—and more than thirty foreign royal guests, representing the Hellenes, Denmark, Norway, Roumania, Sweden, the Netherlands, Spain, Luxemburg, Belgium and Iraq.

Later that day, as dusk descended, Princess Elizabeth and the Duke of Edinburgh set out at the start of their honeymoon spent in Hampshire at Broadlands, the home of the bridegroom's uncle, 'Dickie' Mountbatten. It was there, indeed, that the Princess received a touching letter from her father: 'I was so proud of you and thrilled at having you so close to me on our long walk in Westminster Abbey,' the King wrote, 'but when I handed your hand to the Archbishop, I felt I had lost something very precious. You were so calm and composed during the Service and said your words with such conviction, that I knew everything was all right.'

The Duke and Duchess of Edinburgh's first married home had been found not far from Windsor, an estate known as Sunninghill Park. Alas, the couple's plans to live there literally went up in smoke when the house was set ablaze, some said by tinkers. The short-term alternative, therefore, was for them to stay on at Buckingham Palace until Clarence House, a later addition to the red-brick Tudor Palace of St James's, further down the Mall, could be refurbished for them. Living 'at home', even in a palace, was far from ideal, as the Princess and her husband realized only too well, but for the time being at least, it was more convenient than, say, temporary accommodation at a royal grace-and-favour property miles from anywhere. Furthermore, Buckingham Palace was infinitely more accessible for the Princess's doctors when, during the spring of 1948, it was confirmed that Her Royal Highness was to have a baby at about the time of her first wedding anniversary.

As it happened Prince Charles was born six days before that date, on 14th November at 9.14 in the evening. As the notice to that effect was framed, ready for hanging on the palace railings, a cheery-voiced policeman cried out to the waiting crowds 'It's a boy!' Inside the house

The christening of Prince Charles, Duke of Cornwall. Princess Elizabeth
holding her infant son sits between the Dowager Marchioness of Milford
Haven and Queen Mary in the White Drawing Room at Buckingham Palace.
Behind stand Lady Brabourne, The Duke of Edinburgh, King George VI,
Sir David Bowes Lyon, the Earl of Athlone (Queen Mary's brother 'Algie')
and Princess Margaret.

the Duke of Edinburgh celebrated by sharing bottles of champagne with his staff and later, as soon as she was comfortably settled, he bounded in to Princess Elizabeth's room carrying a bouquet of roses and carnations.

As Elizabeth Longford tells us in her study *Elizabeth R*, Malcolm Muggeridge, who was to find himself in such hot water a few years later over his article about the young Elizabeth II, was as pleased by the Prince's birth as anyone else and wrote, 'How very much more satisfactory is the institution of monarchy than, for instance, the American presidency, with all the dangers and vulgarities inherent in the process of election.'

To the King and Queen, who had celebrated their silver wedding that April, the birth of their first grandchild was an occasion of overwhelming happiness, while Princess Margaret, on an official visit to Sheffield at the time, joked that from now on she would no doubt be known as 'Charlie's aunt'.

Princess Elizabeth with her son in 1949.

Charles Philip Arthur George, Duke of Cornwall and future Prince of Wales, was christened in the Music Room at Buckingham Palace four weeks after his birth. Among those present that day, 15th December, was the infant's great-grandmother Queen Mary. Dressed in royal blue velvet and as dignified a figure as ever, the eighty-one-year-old Queen Dowager was so proud of the historic significance of her christening gift, that she noted in her journal, 'I gave the baby a silver gilt cup and cover which George III had given to a godson in 1780, so that I gave a present from my great-grandfather to my great-grandson 168 years later.'

If only for a while Prince Charles's birth helped ease the royal family's anxiety over the King's health. Never a robust man, as his early medical records testified only too well, he had been suffering from cramp in both legs from the beginning of 1948. By the end of that year, a numbness made walking uncomfortable and at night, pain in both feet prevented him from sleeping. It was not until then, however, that the King mentioned anything about his gradually deteriorating condition and, when his doctors were finally consulted, they diagnosed arteriosclerosis. The following March he underwent a right lumbar sympathectomy with satisfactory results. But, said the King's surgeons, his hold on life would be frail and, although the decision was his, they strongly advised His Majesty not to tax himself unduly. Swallowing what was a bitter pill, a spring tour of Australia and New Zealand was postponed on the grounds that 'It would be hazardous for His Majesty to embark upon a long journey.'

That June, however, King George VI was as determined as he had ever been to attend the Trooping the Colour ceremony and, despite his condition, insisted upon riding to the parade. It was only with the utmost difficulty that Princess Margaret dissuaded her father from that course and persuaded him to ride in an open landau instead. So it was that Princess Elizabeth took part in her first Trooping ceremony. Dressed in a dark blue uniform, she rode close by her father's carriage. At her next appearance, the blue tunic had been exchanged for scarlet, her peaked forage cap for the now familiar plumed bearskin.

Many changes were in the wind for the Heiress Presumptive as the 1940s came to a close and the new decade opened. In August 1950 the line of succession was reshuffled once more when Princess Elizabeth gave birth to her only daughter, for whom the names Anne Elizabeth Alice Louise were chosen. Little more than a year before, the Princess and the Duke of Edinburgh had finally moved into Clarence House.

**Princess Elizabeth and Prince Charles in the garden of St James's Palace,
await the state procession of the visiting Dutch Queen Juliana, 1950.**

The date was 4th July and, for more than one reason, did the Duke jokingly refer to it as 'Independence Day'. It was at Clarence House that Princess Anne was born at 11.50 a.m. on 15th August, and among her first visitors was Queen Elizabeth. Looking down at the 6lb infant as she slept, the Queen remarked with grandmotherly pride, 'Isn't she lovely!'

Throughout the next eighteen months still more official duties devolved upon Princess Elizabeth, many of them functions her father was unable to fulfil. Though it is said he knew nothing about it, the King had developed cancer, and in September 1951 his left lung was removed. The following month his elder daughter flew out of London at the start of a long arranged official visit to Canada and the United States, and among the paperwork she necessarily took with her was a sealed envelope which—just in case—contained her Accession documents. On that occasion they were not required. Four months later,

however, as the Princess and the Duke of Edinburgh began a journey to Australia and New Zealand, representing the King on the tour he had had to put off, they were.

On 5th February 1952, George VI greatly enjoyed a day's shooting on the Sandringham estate, remaining in high spirits for the rest of the day. Queen Elizabeth and Princess Margaret returned from a visit to Edward Seago, a painter whose work they much admired, with a few canvases for the King to look at. At dinner His Majesty was contented and relaxed with his wife, his younger daughter and their guests, and later he put on the radio ('the wireless') to listen to the latest reports from Kenya about the first leg of Princess Elizabeth's tour. Then, at about 10.30 p.m., laughing heartily at a joke he had just heard, as Princess Margaret recalls, he said goodnight and went off to his room. At about midnight the King was seen at his window, fastening the latch. Sometime during the small hours of that morning, 6th February, George VI died in his sleep.

At the moment of her accession Princess Elizabeth, or Queen Elizabeth II as she had now become, was perched high in a wild fig-tree, the giant *mgumu*, in the original Treetops Hotel. There, surrounded by forest, a salt-lick and a large pool which could be lit to simulate moonlight attracted a host of creatures from elephants and rhino to warthogs and Colobus monkeys. Enthralled by all she saw, Princess Elizabeth filmed the extraordinary scenes below with a cine-camera, the celluloid images doubtless intended to be 'premiered' before the King and Queen soon after her return home.

Thirty-one years later, during a return visit to Kenya, the Queen and Prince Philip made a sentimental pilgrimage to the site of Treetops. Although remarkably adept at not allowing herself to betray inner feelings in public, the Queen's profound disappointment at what she saw was unmistakable. The original wooden building from which she had filmed the wildlife had been burned down by the Mau-Mau and had been replaced, though on the opposite bank of the pond, by a much bigger structure, high on stilts, which spoke too loudly of the slick and not altogether appealing commercialism of the 1980s. Moreover, the forest had been cleared rendering it so unrecognizable that Her Majesty had to ask her husband in disbelief, 'Was this where we came before?'

In 1952 the idyllic spell of Treetops had been broken by the very first unconfirmed stories of the King's demise. The Duke of Edinburgh was told by his equerry Michael Parker who said later, 'I

never felt so sorry for anyone in all my life. He looked as if you'd dropped half the world on him.' While the rest of the royal party waited on official news from London, the Duke took his wife out to inspect the horses that had been selected for a ride, originally planned for the following day. Two hours later Parker drew Prince Philip aside to tell him that confirmation had finally been received.

Pale but composed, the new Queen broke the seal on the envelope she had hoped would not be required, and immediately attended to her first duties as sovereign, the despatch of letters and telegrams to the governors and heads of government over which she now reigned.

Late the following afternoon it was only once the aircraft bearing the royal party had touched down at London Airport that the Queen could face putting on the black coat and hat of mourning that had been brought back from Mombasa, where the travellers were to have joined the liner *Gothic* for the next stage of their tour. Looking out of the plane's windows at the line of official Daimler limousines, the young sovereign said quietly, 'Oh, they've sent those hearses.' It was a term she and her sister had always jokingly used when referring to the state cars. Now, in the gathering gloom of that February afternoon, the expression assumed a new meaning and acted as a sudden, oppressive reminder of all that now lay ahead.

Accompanied by Lord and Lady Mountbatten, the Duke of Gloucester (the late King's younger brother, Prince Henry) boarded the aircraft to spend a few minutes alone with the Queen and her consort, before they disembarked to be greeted by representatives of Her Majesty's Privy Council. First the Prime Minister, Winston Churchill, who bowed his head to his sovereign with tears rolling down his cheeks, then the former Labour premier, Clement Attlee, followed by the Foreign Secretary, Anthony Eden.

With the inevitable formalities over, the Queen drove home to Clarence House where she was met by Queen Mary. 'Her old Grannie and subject must be the first to kiss her hand', she said as she prepared to take the short drive from Marlborough House.

Next morning, while the Proclamation of her accession was ceremoniously announced throughout the kingdom, Elizabeth II journeyed to Sandringham to join her mother.

CHAPTER FOUR

UNDOUBTED QUEEN

The first state occasion of the young Queen Elizabeth's reign was the funeral of her father at St George's Chapel, Windsor. For three days and four nights beforehand, George VI had lain in state at Westminster Hall, during which time no fewer than 305,806 ordinary men and women filed past the high purple catafalque on which the King's coffin rested.

Interred among his ancestors on 15th February 1952, following the slow and sombre journey from London, it fell to the Queen to sprinkle earth from a silver dish as the words of the committal were read and the remains of the third sovereign of the Royal House of Windsor were lowered to the tombhouse beneath the choir.

That November Elizabeth II presided over a happier, but no less impressive, ceremony when she rode in state to Westminster to open Parliament for the first time. Dressed in gold lace with the scarlet velvet robe worn by the young Queen Victoria cascading from her shoulders, Her Majesty rested her left hand on her consort's right hand as, with great dignity, she walked between the rows of onlookers thronging the Royal Gallery towards the Upper Chamber. There the Queen read aloud the declaration of faith and then, in 'clear and well-modulated tones' addressed her first 'Gracious Speech' to the highest assembly in the land. On this occasion, however, tradition prevented the Queen from wearing the Imperial State Crown. That honour could only be accorded after her coronation, indisputably the single most important ceremony in the life of any British sovereign, which at that time, still lay seven months hence.

In all, sixteen months separated the Queen's accession from her coronation, a period which not only allowed full court mourning to be observed and private grief to subside rather more, but provided sufficient time for the Duke of Norfolk, the hereditary Earl Marshal, to mastermind the entire Ceremonial with total precision.

At Westminster Abbey Ministry of Works' builders and carpenters completely transformed the ancient interior. Over the sacrarium, normally dominated by the High Altar, a huge, gold-carpeted platform was constructed. On it, beneath the Royal Gallery, set as before over the tomb of Henry VIII's fourth wife, Anne of Cleves, were placed the Chair of Estate, the six hundred and fifty year old St (or King) Edward's Chair, by tradition the 'Coronation Chair', in

RIGHT: **The funeral of King George VI, February 1952.**

which the sovereign is actually crowned and, beyond that, facing the altar and set on a dais approached on all sides by five deep steps, the Throne. Gilded and covered in rose brocade, emblazoned with the Queen's cipher, it was here that the Dukes of Edinburgh, Gloucester and Kent, the Archbishop of Canterbury and the High Officers of State would declare allegiance, each swearing to become Her Majesty's 'liege man of life and limb, and of earthly worship; and faith and truth . . . to live and die, against all manner of folks'.

All along the nave, on three sides of Poets' Corner and the north transept, sometimes called 'The Statesmen's Aisle', which looked down on to the 'Coronation Theatre', vast, tiered galleries—faced with silk brocade—were built to accommodate the congregation to be numbered on the day in their thousands. Beyond the west door and extending out into the street known as Broad Sanctuary, a special annexe was built. Through it the Queen would enter and depart.

Described as 'an exceptionally light, airy and spacious chamber', one entire wall was made of white frosted glass, with every alternate pane bearing a sand-blasted floral emblem—either rose, thistle, shamrock or leek. The ceiling, 'a splendid red, sown with gold stars, the carpet blue, the walls oyster white'. Draped across the entrance to the Queen's Retiring Room, prepared with every necessary facility from lavatories to a dining-room, were oyster silk curtains, opposite which stood a richly caparisoned table bearing the royal regalia—in other words, the Crown Jewels. Stationed in this 'Chamber' were the twenty-one Yeoman Warders from the Tower of London, traditional guardians of the regalia, whose number on this occasion was to be supplemented by fifty officers and men of the Queen's Company, the Grenadier Guards.

Elsewhere preparations were also proceeding with feverish industry. In their workroom craftsmen from Garrards, the Crown Jewellers, were cleaning the gems and refitting the frame of the State Crown; in Bruton Street Norman Hartnell and his team were not only creating the gown to be worn by the Queen herself, but those of her six maids-of-honour, and of several royal ladies, included among them Queen Elizabeth The Queen Mother (as George VI's widow had chosen to be known), Princess Margaret, the Duchess of Kent and Princess Alexandra.

Streets, too, were being adorned with all kinds of decorations. Stretching away from Buckingham Palace down the length of the Mall, stands for spectators and bannered flag-staffs were erected,

while overhead soared intricate triumphal arches interspersed with vast, metal-work crowns, seemingly suspended in mid-air, all of which were brilliantly floodlit at night. In the centre of Piccadilly Circus, the statue of Eros, a memorial to the great Lord Shaftesbury, was surrounded by a towering 'golden cage', studded with tiny light bulbs, while in Oxford Street, Selfridges—renowned for staging the most sumptuous pageants on such occasions—adopted a theme which spanned four centuries and linked Queen Elizabeth I with Queen Elizabeth II. Set between two pillars above the store's main entrance, the display's *pièce de résistance* was a grand-scale equestrian statue of the new Queen, shown riding to the Sovereign's Birthday Parade. Set behind it was a full-length portrait of 'Good Queen Bess', while flanking the whole were panels bearing extracts from speeches made by the respective monarchs in 1558 and 1953.

In the Royal Mews at Buckingham Palace all the state coaches and carriages were being overhauled in readiness for the kind of procession that would not be seen again until the celebration of the Queen's Silver Jubilee, at that time twenty-four years distant. Most spectacular of all the royal conveyances was (and still is) the great Gold State Coach which, until the late 1930s, was not only used to transport the sovereign to his or her coronation, but to open Parliament as well. Indeed, on just such an occasion was this monumental coach first seen when, on 25th November 1762, King George III rode in it to Westminster.

Twenty-four feet long, eight feet and three inches wide, twelve feet high and weighing four tons, eight horses are required to draw it. A full description of the State Coach, 'the most superb and expensive of any ever built in this Kingdom', tells us that: 'The framework consists of eight palm trees which, branching at their tops, support the roof. The four corner trees, each rising from a lion's head, are loaded with trophies symbolizing the victories of Great Britain in the Seven Years War that had ended shortly before the coach was completed.'

The body of the coach is slung by braces covered in morocco leather and ornamented with gilt buckles held by four tritons. The two front figures draw the coach—cables attached to cranes are stretched over their shoulders—and they proclaim the approach of the Monarch of the Ocean through conch shells used as trumpets or horns. The rear figures carry the Imperial fasces (bundles of rods carried before the high magistrate as emblems of authority) topped with tridents. On the centre of the roof stand three cherubs. Representing the genii of

England, Scotland and Ireland, they support the Royal Crown and hold in their hands the Sceptre, the Sword of State, and the Ensign of Knighthood. Their bodies are draped with festoons of laurel which trail off to the four corners of the roof. The driver's footboard (although the coach is no longer driven) is shaped as a large scallop shell adorned with reeds, the pole fashioned to represent a bundle of lances, and the wheels representative of those on ancient triumphal cars.

Adding to the overall magnificence of the State Coach are the door, side, front and back panels which were painted by Giovanni Battista Cipriani (a Florentine historical painter and engraver) who came to London in 1755.

Rehearsals of the actual coronation ceremony were held at West-minster Abbey for all those who were to participate in the processions and, of course, in the service, itself, while in the long Picture Gallery at Buckingham Palace—a sheet attached to her shoulders—the Queen practised walking the length of an imaginary 'nave', her maids of honour familiarizing themselves with the pace at which they, too, had to walk, supporting the weighty trains of the robes Her Majesty would wear.

Following a precedent established by her mother-in-law in 1937 when she attended the coronation of King George VI, Queen Elizabeth The Queen Mother indicated that she naturally wished to be present at the crowning of her daughter. But for Queen Mary history would not, alas, repeat itself. On 24th March, nine weeks before the day of the coronation and shortly before her eighty-sixth birthday, the old Queen Dowager died peacefully at Marlborough House.

Once more the beat of muffled funeral drums and the sound of slowly marching feet filled the silent streets, as a gun-carriage bore the body of George V's revered Queen to Westminster Hall to lie in state. Once more did the royal womenfolk put on their black mourning veils, and once more did the young Queen Elizabeth sprinkle earth from a silver dish onto the coffin as it was lowered into the royal vault at St George's Chapel.

To both the Queen and Princess Margaret, Queen Mary had seemed a severe figure in their lives. Though there is no doubt that she held enormous affection for her granddaughters, the old Queen had rarely been at ease in the company of her own sex and her aloof, even

In March 1953, the young Queen, heavily veiled once more, drives away
from Westminster Hall with the Duke of Edinburgh, having attended the
lying-in-state of her grandmother Queen Mary.

distant, manner unwittingly instilled fear in both the Princesses as
they were growing up. That feeling remains with them to this day.
Among Queen Mary's last wishes, however, was one which paid a
loving tribute to Elizabeth II. It was simply that her death, should it
occur before, must not be allowed to interfere in any way with the
plans for the coronation. That wish was honoured.

————————————————

Tuesday, 2nd June 1953 was a day of intermittent, if prolonged and
heavy, showers. It had rained on the Queen's wedding-day five and a
half years before, and it would rain on 7th June 1977, when the nation
paid tribute to the Queen on her Silver Jubilee. Yet if all else became
uncomfortably dank, nothing could wet the enthusiasm of the good
nature of tens of thousands who turned out to cheer the Queen on each
occasion.

On Coronation Day no available space along the entire processional

April 1953: the Queen and the Duke of Edinburgh, Princess Margaret
and the Princess Royal attend the Badminton Horse Trials. In the
background (with pocket handkerchief) is Group Captain Peter Townsend
with whom the Queen's sister was already in love and whose story
would soon become world news.

route was left unoccupied. Literally millions of people were crammed cheek by jowl into streets through which the Queen would pass. Simply 'being there' was enough for a multitude, who held little hope of glimpsing very much over the heads of all the densely packed rows in front of them. All London, or so it seemed, had been 'up and doing' since long before dawn broke. 'The day of days' enthused 'Chips' Channon when he awoke at 4.15 a.m. and prepared himself for the day ahead. Four hours later, having taken his seat at Westminster Abbey, Channon watched the great church come to vibrant life as the vast congregation began to arrive dressed in all manner of finery—cloaked peers clutching coronets (in which many had secreted packets of sandwiches to be consumed during the 'interval'), peeresses in trailing red velvet over glittering evening dresses, Commonwealth representatives, ambassadors, assorted diplomats and foreign royalties. In a dazzling array of uniforms and decorations, silks, satins, furs and diamonds, the processions unfurled. The huge frame of Salote, Queen of the small Pacific island kingdom of Tonga, a jovial and highly popular figure who clearly enjoyed riding unshielded in an open carriage despite the rain, was perhaps the most colourful of overseas visitors.

Certainly Queen Salote, dark-skinned and clad in vivid pink, succeeded in delighting the crowds who cheered as she waved and grinned expansively in response to their welcome. 'Who is that with her?' somebody is reputed to have asked Noël Coward, referring to the small, slight man in a black top hat riding in her carriage. 'Her lunch!' Coward replied sardonically.

Less exotic royal figures who gathered in London at the Queen's invitation included Crown Prince Olav (now King) of Norway and his wife the Crown Princess Märtha, Prince Bernhard of the Netherlands, Prince Albert of Liège, brother of the Belgian King, Prince Axel and Princess Margaretha of Denmark, Prince Bertil of Sweden, Prince Akihito of Japan, the Emir Abdul Illah of Iraq, Prince Buu Loc of Vietnam, and Prince Chula Chakrabongse of Thailand.

As protocol demands, members of the British royal family arrived at Westminster Abbey in order of precedence: the Duchess of Kent with her children, the Duchess of Gloucester with her sons William and Richard, the Princess Royal, and then Princess Margaret who preceded Queen Elizabeth The Queen Mother, whose purple mantle had been worn to the last coronation by Queen Mary.

Finally the tumultuous sounds beyond the abbey walls told the

ABOVE: Coronation Day, 2nd June 1953: Elizabeth II and her consort ride to Westminster Abbey in the State Coach, originally built for King George III.

RIGHT: A view of the State Coach making its way towards Westminster.

congregation that the Queen herself had at last arrived. As she stepped down from the State Coach to be greeted by the Duke of Norfolk, footmen assisted three of the maids-of-honour, Lady Anne Coke, Lady Mary Baillie-Hamilton and Lady Jane Heathcote-Drummond-Willoughby, with Her Majesty's train. Then, with consummate grace, the sovereign entered the glass-walled annexe. 'The Queen was so wonderfully calm', remembers Lady Anne Coke (now Lady Glenconner, lady-in-waiting to Princess Margaret), 'that she made us feel calm too. We [the maids of honour] were all very excited and very nervous. But the Queen had a marvellous serenity about her.'

Attended by her pages and mistress of the robes, Queen Elizabeth The Queen Mother crosses the Coronation Theatre. Among the guests (second row left) seated in the Choir Stalls is the future Indian Prime Minister Indira Gandhi.

Inside the annexe the Queen put down the bouquet of roses and lily-of-the-valley that she had carried with her from Buckingham Palace, while Norman Hartnell darted to and fro arranging the floor-length gown that Her Majesty had called 'simply glorious'. Of white

satin, the crystal-embroidered bodice flared into a full skirt intricately worked in gold, silver and crystal, upon which, in subtle shades of pink, blue, yellow and green, the rose, thistle, leek and shamrock (emblems of England, Scotland, Wales and Northern Ireland, respectively) had been delicately hand-sewn.

Behind the Queen her six maids formed up. Wearing identical dresses of white satin with a gold motif ('Very beautiful', said Anne Glenconner, 'but because they were not lined the embroidery tended to prickle') they were followed by the then Mistress of the Robes, the Dowager Duchess of Devonshire, then the Ladies of the Bedchamber (none of whom, by rank, can be anything less than Countesses) and the Women of the Bedchamber—collectively known as Ladies-in-waiting.

As Her Majesty approached the west door the choir broke into song, performing Psalm 122, 'I was glad when they said unto me, We will go into the house of the Lord.' Slowly the procession moved along the nave, through the arch of the ornate organ screen, thence to the Coronation Theatre where the Queen went to her Chair of Estate. One by one the Lords brought in the Regalia and delivered them to the Dean of Westminster who placed them upon the altar. The ceremony had now begun and the Queen moved to St Edward's Chair for the Recognition. To each of the four sides of the abbey, the Archbishop of Canterbury, flanked by the Lord Chancellor, the Lord Great Chamberlain, the Lord High Constable and the Earl Marshal, and preceded by Garter King-of-Arms, charged the congregation: 'Sirs, I here present unto you QUEEN ELIZABETH, your Undoubted Queen: Wherefore all you who are come this day to do your homage and service, Are you willing to do the same?'

Each time the congregation roared in reply, 'God Save Queen Elizabeth', and each time the Recognition was greeted with a fanfare of trumpets. Having then returned to the Chair of Estate, the Archbishop stepped forward to administer the Coronation Oath.

'Madam, is Your Majesty willing to take the Oath?' he asked.

'I am willing', the Queen quietly replied.

'Will you solemnly promise and swear to govern the Peoples of the United Kingdom of Great Britain and Northern Ireland ... and of your Possessions and other Territories to any of them belonging or pertaining, according to their respective laws and customs?'

'I solemnly promise so to do', the Queen responded.

'Will you to the utmost of your power maintain the Laws of God

and the true profession of the Gospel? Will you to the utmost of your power maintain in the United Kingdom the Protestant Reformed Religion established by law? Will you maintain and preserve inviolably the settlement of the Church of England, and the doctrine, worship, discipline, and government thereof, as by law established in England? And will you preserve unto the Bishops and Clergy of England, and to the Churches there committed to their charge, all such rights and privileges, as by law do or shall appertain to them or any of them?'

'All this I promise to do', Her Majesty replied and then with a hand placed on a Bible brought from the high altar, the Queen said, 'The things which I have here before promised, I will perform and keep. So help me God.'

The Queen has been crowned and the Duke of Edinburgh has put on his own coronet.

Later in the service came the moment of Anointing when, in a ceremony that traces its origins to Biblical days, the sovereign's hands, breast and head were anointed with 'Holy Oil'. As the anthem 'Zadok the Priest and Nathan the Prophet' was sung, the Mistress of the Robes helped the Queen put on a simple white dress known as the Colobium Sindonis. Then, with Her Majesty seated in St Edward's

Souvenirs of the Silver Jubilee of King George V and Queen Mary in 1935,
and the Coronation of King George VI and Queen Elizabeth, two years
later.

TOP: Persuaded by Princess Margaret to do so, King George VI drove
to the 1949 Trooping the Colour ceremony in a semi-state landau.

ABOVE: Her Majesty Queen Elizabeth II. A formal portrait by Cecil Beaton.

ABOVE LEFT: A fashionable Princess Elizabeth attends a fête in Windsor Great Park.

LEFT: Flags, tins of biscuits, hair-grips, tea caddies, packets of sewing needles and handkerchief bearing the young Queen's likeness were mass produced to celebrate Her Majesty's Coronation, 2nd June 1953.

RIGHT: The royal party at Badminton in 1953.

BELOW: Prince Charles at play in the garden of Clarence House.

Chair, a canopy of cloth-of-gold was held over her by four Knights of the Garter. Oil was poured from the Ampulla and with it, making the sign of the cross on the Queen's hands, the Archbishop said, 'Be thy Hands anointed with holy Oil.' Then, 'Be thy Breast anointed with holy Oil', and lastly, 'Be thy Head anointed with holy Oil; as Kings, priests and prophets were anointed . . .'.

As the canopy was taken away the Queen was invested with the golden Supertunica, the first of two further robes custom decreed she must wear. Thus arrayed, the Regalia were presented: the Sword; the Armills (or the Bracelets) of sincerity and wisdom; the Royal (or Dalmatic) Robe, representing the robe of righteousness; the Orb with the Cross, symbolizing the world subjected to 'the Power and Empire of Christ'. Then was presented the Ring of Kingly Dignity (a large sapphire surrounded with diamonds and set with a cross of rubies); the Sceptre with the Cross, 'the ensign of power and justice'; the Rod with the Dove (representing equity and mercy), then finally, the Crown of St Edward. As it was placed on to the Queen's head the Princes and Princesses of the Blood and the Peers and Peeresses put on their own coronets and, as the congregation repeatedly shouted GOD SAVE THE QUEEN, canon salutes were fired from the Tower of London, proclaiming that Elizabeth II was crowned!

Subsequent ceremonies of Benediction, Enthronement and Homage then preceded the Act of Communion and finally, as the coronation was concluded, the Queen retired to the Chapel of St Edward the Confessor, which lies immediately behind the High Altar. There, as the 'Te Deum' was sung, the Queen was divested of St Edward's Crown and the symbolic garments. Now, standing before a full-length mirror, she put on the magnificent 120-year-old Imperial State Crown, containing the Black Prince's ruby, St Edward's sapphire, and the Second Star of Africa (a diamond of 317. 40 metric carats, cut from the Cullinan Diamond which is set in the Sceptre with the Cross). Apart from these stones, the Crown contains four rubies, seventeen sapphires, eleven emeralds, 277 pearls and some 3,000 diamonds.

Last of all Her Majesty was arrayed in the Imperial Robe of State. Made of heavy silk-lined purple velvet and embroidered with her cypher, it was trimmed with ermine and, at the shoulders, golden tassels and white satin bows. Once again the maids-of-honour took up their places to support the weight of the train and, as a fanfare of trumpets filled the abbey and the National Anthem was sung, the

LEFT: The Queen is seated in the Chair of Estate at the start of the long coronation ceremony. Near her stand her six maids-of-honour while in the Royal Gallery, set over the tomb of Anne of Cleves, are: (front row, left to right) Princess Alexandra of Kent, the Duchess of Kent, the Princess Royal, Queen Elizabeth The Queen Mother, the Princess Margaret, Prince William of Gloucester, the Duchess of Gloucester and her second son Prince Richard. In the row behind, wearing the grey habit of the religious order she founded, is Princess Andrew of Greece, mother of the Duke of Edinburgh.

ABOVE: The State Coach conveying Her Majesty and the Duke of Edinburgh back to Buckingham Palace.

Queen's procession began its stately progress down through the body of the church to the annexe, thence out to the waiting State Coach and the acclamation of the people.

The long procession slowly wound its way through London, riding through snatches of sunshine, rain and hail. Up Whitehall came the coaches and their mounted escorts to Trafalgar Square, then to St James's Street, Piccadilly, through Hyde Park, Oxford Street and Regent Street, back to Trafalgar Square and then, at long last, into the Mall. Though the Queen's procession passed by without interruption, to a welcome that can only be described as ecstatic, a few hitches did occur elsewhere. Winston Churchill's carriage had to be pushed to one side when a fault interrupted its journey in Trafalgar Square, while the carriage containing Princess Alice and the Earl of Athlone suddenly stopped dead at Hyde Park Corner, its wheels skidding on a slight, but rain-sodden, incline. Three policemen rushed forward to help it back on its way, which enabled the rest of the halted procession—including Queen Elizabeth The Queen Mother and Princess Margaret riding in the Irish State Coach—to continue.

Precisely six hours and twenty-nine minutes after she had set out for Westminster Abbey the Queen returned to Buckingham Palace, and with the excited crowds massed below Her Majesty and her attendants, together with the entire royal family, appeared again and again on the scarlet and gold draped balcony.

'That scene is one I shall never forget', said Lady Glenconner. 'The Mall was just one vast mass of cheering people.'

Almost immediately the Queen and the Duke of Edinburgh embarked on an arduous programme of 'Coronation' engagements. In an open-topped Rolls-Royce they undertook a series of state drives through all the districts of which London is composed. On the evening of 8th June the royal couple, accompanied by members of their family, attended a gala evening at the Royal Opera House, Covent Garden, when Benjamin Britten's opera 'Gloriana'—which tells the story of Elizabeth I and the Earl of Essex—was performed. To many an acquired taste, Britten's opera was not, perhaps, the wisest choice. Indeed Noël

RIGHT: Divested of her robe and the royal insignia, save the magnificent Imperial State Crown, the Queen makes a solo appearance on the palace balcony.

The Queen and members of the royal party watch the fly-past from the balcony of Buckingham Palace.

Coward, the acknowledged 'Master' of light, often highly sophisticated entertainment, considered it ' . . . a bugger. Dull, without melody as usual with Mr B., and not happily chosen'.

One week later the Queen, as Lord High Admiral, attended the customary Review of the Fleet at Spithead, and during the following weeks undertook coronation visits to Scotland, Northern Ireland and Wales, respectively, winding up her schedule at Odiham on 15th July, where Her Majesty witnessed the Coronation Review of the Royal Air Force.

Four months later came the start of the mammoth coronation tour of the Commonwealth, during which it was estimated that the Queen heard the National Anthem sung in full 508 times, had listened to 276 speeches and had herself delivered 102, had been curtsied to 6,770 times, had shaken hands with 13,213 individuals, and had received almost 200 substantial gifts.

Could there have been any doubt that the reign of Queen Elizabeth II had begun in earnest?

CHAPTER FIVE

WITHIN A FAMILY CIRCLE

During the 1950s there were few particularly outstanding events in the official life of the royal family. As Head of State, the Queen had begun to receive state visitors—the earliest being King Gustav VI Adolf of Sweden, and the 'Lion of Judah', otherwise Haile Selassie, Emperor of Ethiopia—and had started to undertake visits of a like nature herself. In June 1955 she paid a sovereign-to-sovereign call upon King Haakon VII of Norway and the following year returned the Swedish King's visit. In 1957 Her Majesty was received in Portugal, France and Denmark, and in October that year she visited New York to address the United Nations assembly. Five months later the Queen spent two days in the Netherlands as the guest of her 'sister sovereign', Queen Juliana.

Setting aside the business of State Visits, however, which the Duke of Windsor—as Prince of Wales and as King—regarded as 'rot . . . a waste of time, money and energy', the media homed in on rumours of a rift between the Queen and her husband. The couple had, in fact, hit a patch of turbulence in their marriage but, in the haughty, tight-lipped manner royal 'officialdom' always adopts when worried, the rumours and headline stories were all hotly denied and subsequently ignored.

Nevertheless the theme of love and marriage had occupied Fleet Street's time for two years—1953 to 1955—when it was revealed that the beautiful and vivacious Princess Margaret, then in her twenties, had fallen in love with, and wanted to marry, her father's former equerry, Group Captain Peter Townsend. This débacle all but stole the Queen's thunder and, in turn, gave rise to rumours of another 'rift'—this time between the royal sisters. The truth of the matter was that the Queen herself was delighted at her sister's happiness, but by virtue of her position as Head of the Church was rendered powerless to aid Princess Margaret's cause.

In a nut-shell, Peter Townsend was the innocent party in the divorce action he had brought against his wife Rosemary. But since divorce, especially in those unenlightened days, totally opposed the Church's 'teachings' Townsend was seen as anything but a suitable candidate for the hand of the Queen's only sister. That said, both Princess Margaret and the Group Captain had been told that marriage was not impossible; they were assured that something could be arranged. At the end of the day, however, no strings had been pulled

RIGHT: At Buckingham Palace Princess Elizabeth cradles her daughter who has just been christened Anne Elizabeth Alice Louise.

LEFT: Princess Elizabeth and the Duke of Edinburgh at Clarence House with Prince Charles and the infant Princess Anne—1950.

RIGHT: Prince Charles, a pupil at Hill House School, boards a hired bus on the school's sports day.

FAR RIGHT: The Queen Mother with her grandchildren at a window of Clarence House on Her Majesty's 55th birthday—4th August 1955.

BELOW: Princess Anne puts her fingers to her father's lips in this informal family picture.

and nobody had been won over. The Church, the Cabinet and the Dominion premiers all refused to countenance the marriage, so that after two years of exercising the utmost patience, the Princess and Townsend were no further forward than they had been in 1953, when they had first declared their love for one another before the Queen.

In the circumstances, the only alternative was for Princess Margaret to renounce her right of inheritance and, as her uncle had been forced to do in 1936, leave Britain. That the Princess did not adopt that course was due almost entirely to Group Captain Townsend's decision to rescind his proposal of marriage. The sacrifice for the Princess he said, was too great; the future too uncertain.

So it was that, on 31st October 1955, Princess Margaret issued a statement in which she declared that being, 'mindful of the Church's teachings that Christian marriage is indissoluble', she had decided not to marry Peter Townsend. Twenty-three years later, the desperate irony behind Princess Margaret's decision was to be tragically revealed.

If the Queen's position in relation to the Church meant that she had officially to distance herself from Princess Margaret's dilemma, nothing could prevent her involvement in helping to decide the course of her young son's formal education. As we have already seen, there was no question of any but a private education for the daughters of King George VI. All four of Elizabeth II's children, however, were to experience life at 'proper' schools in their turn and, accordingly, Hill House Preparatory School in salubrious Knightsbridge was chosen to receive the Heir to the Throne in 1956. It was not, of course, a decision that had been taken lightly and, indeed, very many factors had been carefully weighed in the balance. One of them was the vigilant eye of the press. In an attempt to nip that often aggravating presence in the bud, letters were sent from Buckingham Palace to all newspaper editors.

'Her Majesty and the Duke of Edinburgh have decided that their son has reached the stage when he should take part in more grown-up educational pursuits', the editors were told. 'The Queen trusts, therefore, that His Royal Highness will be able to enjoy this in the same way as other children without the embarrassment of constant publicity.'

The Queen's 'trust' was misplaced. For the novelty value of a

Prince Philip taking part in the ceremony
of Crossing the Line during the royal tour
of 1956.

prince, the son of the reigning sovereign, attending school along with other children was not something that could be regarded as an 'ordinary' occurrence. Thus Her Majesty's hopes that Fleet Street might come to ignore the small boy in the familiar uniform of yellow sweater and rust trousers were held in vain.

The same was true a year later when, following in his father's footsteps, Prince Charles went off—as a 'boarder'—to Cheam School in the village of Headley, near the Hampshire Downs. For the Queen

there were a few private tears and the same pangs any mother would experience at the prospect of losing an adored child, at least during term-time, to a 'system' as alien to her as it was to him. To begin with the Prince's misery was clear; the only familiar sight around him taking the form of his personal Scotland Yard detective. Otherwise, as the Headmaster had been instructed, 'It is the wish of the Queen and Prince Philip that there shall be no alteration in the way the school is run and that Prince Charles shall be treated the same as other boys.'

Being treated the same meant sharing a small, uncarpeted dormitory where the Prince had to make his own bed, keep his clothes neatly in a wicker basket, polish his own shoes and help wait at table. There was also a compulsory letter to be written home to his parents—a minimum of one letter per week.

Over and above all such adjustments as these—and it wasn't long before Prince Charles settled in at Cheam: his first end-of-term report told his parents, 'He is still a little shy, but very popular . . .'—the unwelcome attentions of journalists resulted in an assembly of newspaper editors at Buckingham Palace. There the Queen's press secretary, at the time Richard Colville, outlined the disruption continually caused by the press, and laid an ultimatum squarely on the table. Fleet Street either restricted its coverage of the schoolboy Prince to 'stories of genuine significance', or Her Majesty would abandon the plan of educating him in a way most suited to the times. The message finally got through.

Within the year an announcement made by the Queen presented the media with an item that was genuinely significant. Unable to attend the closing ceremony of the British Empire and Commonwealth Games held in Cardiff during the summer of 1958 personally, the Queen sent a recorded message which was relayed over the public address system. Preceded by a short speech—delivered in person by Prince Philip—Her Majesty said:

> 'I want to take this opportunity of speaking to all Welsh people, not only in this arena, but wherever they may be. The British Empire and Commonwealth Games in the capital, together with all the activities of the Festival of Wales, have made this a memorable year for the principality. I have therefore decided to mark it further by an act which will, I hope, give as much pleasure to all Welshmen as it does to me. I intend to create my son Charles Prince of Wales today. When he is grown up, I will present him to you at Caernarvon.'

At that time the Prince's formal 'presentation' still lay a long way

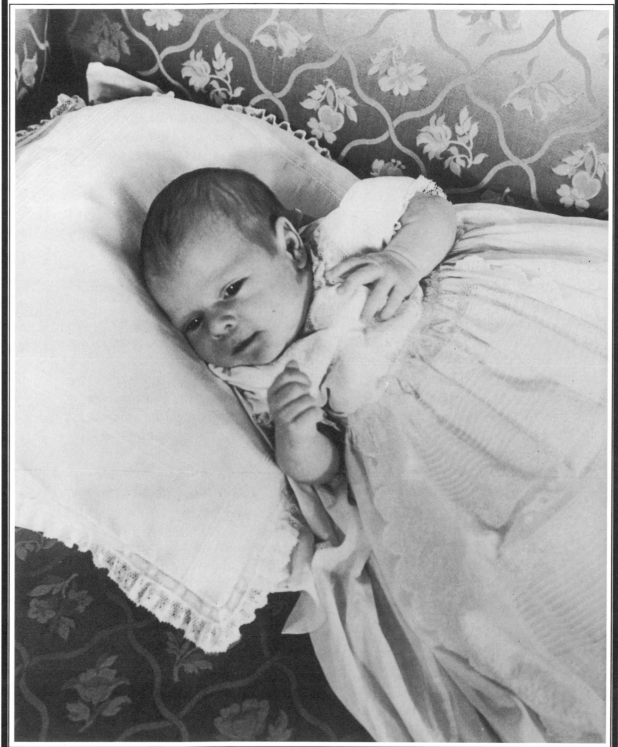

Prince Andrew—the first child to be born to a reigning sovereign
since the days of Queen Victoria—photographed at one month.

off, but when his Investiture did take place in 1969, it was not—as the Queen may have hoped—to the unanimous delight or satisfaction of all Welsh people. First, however, came the completion of Prince Charles's education. Gordonstoun, another of Prince Philip's old schools, up in the wilds of Scotland, and famous for its tough, spartan regimen, was interrupted by a spell at Geelong in Australia, and was eventually followed by Trinity College, Cambridge, and a mere few weeks at Aberystwyth where, appropriately enough, he was despatched to gain at least a grounding in the Welsh language. Many years later the Prince was to say: 'I defy anybody to learn a language in eight weeks which is really what I had. I did my best and I got to a very basic level, "the cow is under the tree over there by the river", or whatever, and a little bit beyond that, but it was very difficult to be able to converse on that basis with important and interesting people that you meet in Wales.'

History may have been written when the Heir Apparent went off to school, but two events that occurred soon after also made significant contributions to the latter-day history of the Royal House of Windsor.

In the Belgian Suite at Buckingham Palace at 3.30 p.m., on 19 February 1960, the Queen gave birth to her third child and second son—Prince Andrew. Not since the days of Queen Victoria had a child been born to the reigning sovereign and on that February evening the news was broadcast to a delighted nation. Christened in the Music Room two months later, the infant Prince—whom Prince Charles was later to call 'the one with the Robert Redford looks'—received the names Andrew Albert Christian Edward. The first of these names clearly remembered Prince Philip's own father, the late Prince Andrew of Greece and Denmark and, indeed, may also have been chosen because of the very special relationship the Queen enjoyed with her mother-in-law, who was formally known as Princess Andrew. The name 'Albert' not only paid tribute to the Queen's father, whose first name it was, but unconsciously, perhaps, complied with Queen Victoria's wish that her male descendants should be called after her late and, oh, so lamented husband, the Prince Consort. 'Christian' re-introduced into the royal family a name unknown since the death of Queen Victoria's third daughter Helena, who had married Prince Christian of Schleswig-Holstein. Nor should it be overlooked that King Christian IX of Denmark was Prince Philip's great-grandfather.

LEFT: Trooping the Colour: as Princess Elizabeth, Her Majesty wore the scarlet regimental uniform for the first time in 1951. In 1972 the Queen wore a black arm-band on parade as a mark of respect for her uncle the Duke of Windsor, whose death had recently occurred.

ABOVE: At three months the Queen carried her youngest son Prince Edward onto the balcony of Buckingham Palace following the Trooping ceremony, June 1964.

ABOVE: The Queen and the Duke of Edinburgh riding in the
State Coach from Buckingham Palace.

ABOVE RIGHT: Her Majesty with Prince Philip and the
Prince of Wales about to enter St Paul's.

RIGHT: Commemorative memorabilia celebrating
Elizabeth II's Silver Jubilee, 1977.

LEFT: The Glass Coach conveying Princess Margaret, the royal bride of 1960, to her wedding, passing through the courtyard of Horse Guards Parade on its way to Westminster Abbey. The Princess is accompanied by the Duke of Edinburgh who was to give her away at the ceremony.

BELOW: The Investiture of the Prince of Wales at Caernarvon Castle. The royal party leaving the castle after the ceremony on 1st July 1969.

At six months Prince Andrew features in the 60th birthday photographs
of his grandmother, the adoring Queen Elizabeth The Queen Mother.

'Edward' was, of course, a popular family name and one borne by no
fewer than eight Kings of England.

The second event that spring brought Princess Margaret back into
the headlines when, on Friday 6th May, she married society photographer, Antony Armstrong-Jones (soon to become the 1st Earl of
Snowdon). The Princess's marriage to a man who actually worked for
a living, who was known to be somewhat 'Bohemian', and who did not
possess so much as the lowliest title—in short a 'commoner'—made
new inroads into the idea of a 'modern monarchy', and cut right across
all that had formerly been held right and acceptable in the closetted
'world' of British royalty.

Princess Margaret had first met Armstrong-Jones on 20th Feb-

ruary 1958 at a private dinner party given by Lady Elizabeth Cavendish, a close friend as well as a lady-in-waiting to the Princess. Although both considered one another 'charming', they might never have got to know each other, much less have fallen head-over-heels in love, had it not been for another of Princess Margaret's closest friends who commissioned Armstrong-Jones to photograph Her Royal Highness for his private album. The assignment led to further meetings between the couple who, to the absolute delight of both the Queen and the Queen Mother, became privately engaged in December 1959.

When the public announcement was made two months later—on 26th February 1960—friends (and some relations) were horrified, spluttering in sheer disbelief that the Princess and 'Tony' were far too much alike in fiery temperament for their marriage to last.

The royal wedding took place on a day of blue skies and brilliant sunshine. By noon—half an hour after the service began—it had become so hot that several guardsmen, sweltering in tightly-buttoned tunics and bamboo-framed bearskins, joined members of the public at casualty points manned by the St John Ambulance Brigade. The wedding of Princess Margaret was the first to be shown 'live' on television, but the last royal occasion on which London was to be seen *en fête*—courtesy of the then Ministry of Works. In subsequent years banners were the most people expected to see by way of 'official' street decorations.

In May 1960, however, the processional route was alive with vibrant colour. Outside Clarence House, where Princess Margaret lived with her mother, a sixty-foot arch of roses—some real, some artificial—spanned the Mall, while white silk banners, embellished with Tudor roses and the entwined initials of the bride and bridegroom, were suspended from crown-topped flagmasts down the entire length of that famous thoroughfare. Buildings along Whitehall were a mass of white hydrangeas, multi-coloured stock and red roses, flags and bunting, while Parliament Square was studded with masts hung with baskets of pink hydrangeas and marguerites. Elsewhere flourished red, gold and orange tulips and banks of rhododendrons, wisteraria and laburnum.

From Buckingham Palace the royal family set out for Westminster Abbey in the fleet of state and semi-state carriages, although this time there were no foreign royal guests, save for the bride's godmother, Queen Ingrid of Denmark. Other royal families, from the Netherlands, Belgium, Luxemburg, Greece, Norway and Sweden, whose

members were regulars at British royal events, were curiously too busy to attend. The general feeling was that the marriage was not deemed acceptable among the smaller, albeit less significant, monarchies. Be that as it may, the absence of foreign delegations meant that the royal wedding was regarded, almost exclusively, as a *British* event and, although a public holiday was not declared, vast crowds of people—estimated at half a million—snapped up every available place, many of them having arrived days before.

The Queen, accompanied by her mother and the Prince of Wales, leaving Buckingham Palace in Queen Alexandra's State Coach for the wedding of Princess Margaret at Westminster Abbey, 6th May 1960.

LEFT: Princess Margaret and her bridegroom, Antony Armstrong-Jones, pass
along the nave of the abbey after their wedding. They are followed by the Princess's
eight bridesmaids. Princess Anne (left) and Marilyn Wills
are seen framed by the Organ Screen.

This was also the last family wedding at which all the royal ladies
wore ground-length dresses. Most outstanding of all was the Queen in
turquoise blue silk and lace, then Queen Elizabeth The Queen
Mother, shimmering in soft gold lamé and cream osprey feathers,
Princess Marina, Duchess of Kent, in pale yellow organdie, Princess
Alexandra in blue slipper-satin and Queen Ingrid in floral silk.

Beneath the pillared portico of Clarence House, the Glass Coach
and a Captain's Escort of the Household Cavalry awaited the bride and
her brother-in-law, Prince Philip, who was to give her away, while at
the gates television cameras—using innovatory 'zoom lenses' for the
very first time—also waited to beam the first glimpses of Her Royal
Highness into millions of homes, including those of a number of the
bride's friends. That the ceremony was being televised meant, as the
Princess pointed out, 'that those of my friends who couldn't come
could still see it. I loved that idea'.

In her room Princess Margaret put on the exquisite wedding gown
of white silk organza that Norman Hartnell had designed for her and
which, because of its total simplicity, surprised and delighted the
fashion-conscious around the world. With a designer's eye for effect,
the bridegroom himself had suggested a severely plain dress that, in
the Princess's words, 'would act as a foil to my headdress'. That
'headdress' was the magnificent Poltimore diamond tiara which had
been specially acquired for Princess Margaret at auction and to which,
when set around a sleek chignon, was affixed a flowing veil of the finest
silk organza.

Having arrived at Westminster Abbey ahead of time, 'because
Philip kept coming into my room saying, "If you don't hurry up, we'll
be late"', as the Princess recalled, the Duke of Edinburgh led the bride
along the blue-carpeted nave to the steps of the sacrarium. Behind
them followed eight small bridesmaids. The daughters of the bridal
couple's friends and relations, they were Princess Anne, Marilyn
Wills, Catherine Vesey, Angela Nevill, Virginia Fitzroy, Annabel
Rhodes, Rose Nevill and Sarah Lowther, each wearing beribboned
copies of the bride's first ball-gown.

Later that day Princess Margaret (who chose not to add the suffix
'Mrs Antony Armstrong-Jones' to her title) and her husband, set sail

Prince Charles and Princess Anne taking Prince Andrew for a stroll at Balmoral during the summer of 1960

for a Caribbean honeymoon aboard the *Britannia*. Spectacularly moored and 'dressed overall' in the Pool of London, the royal yacht finally slipped anchor just in time to catch the tide. On deck the band of the Royal Marines played 'Oh, What a Beautiful Morning' and, as the giant bascules of Tower Bridge were raised to let the ship pass through, bride and 'groom were saluted by a cacophony of ships' sirens and pealing church bells, sounds which rose above the cheers of the crowds lining the river bank.

Perhaps triggered off by the sheer romance of Princess Margaret's wedding, a rumour was spread that the Queen Mother herself was contemplating marriage. Her prospective 'bridegroom' was alleged to be Sir Arthur Penn, an elderly bachelor who held office as Treasurer to Her Majesty. In the distant past royal widows had been known to re-marry, although the last to have done so was Queen Catherine Parr,

At the gallop: the Queen in a private race along the course at Ascot, in 1961.

sixth wife of King Henry VIII who, in 1547, took as her third husband, Thomas Seymour, Lord Admiral of England, and the brother of Jane Seymour the King's third wife.

Historical precedents aside, Queen Elizabeth, as the Queen Mother is better known within royal and court circles, took an exceptionally dim view of such stories and, angered that the press should have dared to print them, issued a firm denial that she had any intention of re-marrying. The very thought, she told friends, was as offensive to her as it was to the memory of her late husband.

Turning as the occasion demanded from senior to junior members of the royal family, the spotlight briefly alighted on the Duke of Kent in 1961 when, at York Minster on 8th June, he married Miss Katharine Worsley, the only daughter of a local squire. That November the birth of a son—David, Viscount Linley—to Princess Margaret and the, by now, Earl of Snowdon, focused public attention back to Clarence House where the child was born. Almost eighteen

ABOVE: The Queen, Prince Charles and Prince Edward on the East Terrace of Windsor Castle in 1969.

TOP: Prince Andrew playing with one of his mother's corgies.

months later the wedding of Princess Alexandra of Kent to the Honourable Angus Ogilvy, grandson of Queen Mary's devoted friend, Mabell, Countess of Airlie, on 24th April 1963, diverted national interest and, on 20th September that year, Princess Anne made the front pages when she, too, went off to boarding school. That chosen was Benenden in the High Weald of Kent, which catered for the educational requirements of 300 girls.

Yet for all the miscellaneous royal events of the decade, two years in particular stand out as among the most memorable. In the spring of 1964 a spate of royal births found historians metaphorically parting the mists of time to look back to the year 1818, when the querulous sons of George III were finally cajoled into marriage so that the throne could be assured of a legitimate heir. Well over a century later no such unseemly 'race' precipitated the births of sons and daughters to the Queen and Princess Margaret, the Duchess of Kent and Princess Alexandra, though some did wonder whether the births of James Ogilvy on 29th February, Prince Edward on 10th March, Lady Helen Windsor on 28th April and Lady Sarah Armstrong-Jones on 1st May, might not have been due to something other than coincidence.

At Caernarvon Castle on 1st July 1969, came the long-awaited Investiture of Prince Charles as the 21st Prince of Wales. Like the Prince's wedding twelve years later, the Investiture—for all its profound symbolism—put one in mind of a lavish Hollywood production, which might justifiably have been prefaced with the story-teller's immortal words, 'Once upon a time'.

Assisted by the renowned theatrical designer Carl Toms and a team of craftsmen—all of whom were carefully watched by the Earl Marshal, the Duke of Norfolk, who assumed overall control—Lord Snowdon transformed the thirteenth-century shell of Edward I's castle into a magnificent twentieth-century set. The focal point was Toms' circular royal dais centred on the wide, terraced sward of the upper ward. Appropriately constructed from Welsh slate, on which was placed an almost primitive throne, the dais was surmounted by a vast, curved canopy of clear perspex, bearing the Prince's triple feathered emblem made from moulded polystyrene.

With the stage set, the royal family travelled overnight from London aboard the royal train, putting into a security-screened siding near Bangor. The Queen and Prince Philip, Prince Charles, Princess Anne and the Queen Mother, the Gloucesters and the Kents, all assembled at Euston Station, all a little nervous at the prospect of tomorrow. It wasn't the ritual that caused feelings of trepidation, so much as the promise of trouble on the part of Welsh nationalist activists. Rebelling against what it saw as English dominance, *Plaid Cymru*, the National Party of Wales, mounted a crusade against the Investiture and the feudal imposition of a non-Welsh prince. Indeed, in three months, seven bomb incidents had served as a grim reminder of changing attitudes.

On the morning of 1st July, Sir Michael Duff, Lord-Lieutenant of Caernarvon and godfather of Lord Snowdon, entertained the entire royal party to 'champagne and coffee refreshments' at Vaynol, his house overlooking the Menai Straits, patrolled that day by police and military.

'The poor little Queen looked tense and nervous', Duff said afterwards, adding in an altogether different vein, that the lack of suitable vehicles meant he had to send the vegetable van to collect his 'darling Kent family' from the royal train. Seized by fits of nerves Princess Anne and her aunt Princess Margaret, had to 'keep excusing themselves', while the Prince of Wales complained that he saw nothing but himself each time the television set was put on. 'It's always me. I'm getting bored with my face.'

The Investiture was a prime example of the *de*humanizing aspects of the monarchy. It was one of those occasions when private fears had to be kept strictly in check in deference to the demands of duty, no matter the dangers, real, imagined or otherwise. Certainly at Caernarvon Castle all appeared calm and unfussed as, to the applause of 4,000 spectators, the Queen—smiling and unhurried—was escorted to the royal dais by Prince Philip. Then followed the start of the actual ceremonial, when Her Majesty 'commanded' the Earl Marshal 'to direct Garter King-of-Arms to summon His Royal Highness The Prince of Wales to Her Presence'. Thus, from the Chamberlain Tower on the south side of the castle, the Prince walked slowly towards the throne, accompanied by the peers bearing his regalia and preceded by Wales Herald-of-Arms Extraordinary and Chester Herald-of-Arms, the Secretary of State for Wales, George Thomas (now Viscount Tonypandy, former Speaker of the House of Lords), and Garter King-of-Arms.

When the procession had halted before the dais the Letters Patent, couched in the antiquated language of royal proclamations, were read aloud in both English and Welsh, 'Greeting' those present and proclaiming on the Queen's behalf that 'We have made and created

Record time! The Queen joking with her sons Charles and Edward as
they race around the Royal Mews at Windsor on motorized go-karts.

and by these Our Letters do make and create Our most dear Son Charles Philip Arthur George Prince of the United Kingdom of Great Britain and Northern Ireland, Duke of Cornwall and Rothesay, Earl of Carrick, Baron of Renfrew, Lord of the Isles and Great Steward of Scotland PRINCE OF WALES and EARL OF CHESTER . . .'.

Kneeling before his mother Prince Charles then paid homage to the Queen 'on behalf of the Principality of Wales and the Earldom of Chester' in the same words that were used at Her Majesty's coronation sixteen years earlier: 'I Charles, Prince of Wales, do become your liege man of life and limb and of earthly worship and faith and truth I will bear unto you to live and die against all manner of folks.'

When the Queen had finally invested Prince Charles with the items of regalia—in much the same form that is observed at the sovereign's coronation—and had crowned him with a golden coronet, Her Majesty and Prince Philip presented their son to the people assembled outside the castle, first from the Queen's Gate, then from the King's Gate and lastly from a platform constructed in the lower ward. After the final presentation, the royal party retired to the Eagle Tower near the main Water Gate, in readiness for the carriage procession through the streets and, a little later, Her Majesty's return to London.

Although strict security hadn't completely silenced the Welsh nationalists, it had helped to muffle their sounds, and at least at Caernarvon Castle, a royal extravaganza, which had cost £55,000 to put on and had commanded a world-wide television audience of 500 million, was seen to have passed off without incident, much to the Queen's intense relief and that of everybody most directly concerned.

Yet all that aside, and keeping such events in proper perspective, there can be little doubt that the Prince of Wales's Investiture provided a colourful finale to what had been a memorable decade in the lives of the Queen and members of the royal family.

CHAPTER SIX

TOWARDS THE FUTURE

After the ambivalent sixties, the 1970s proved to be years in which the monarchy moved still closer towards the people. The novelty of the Queen's first 'walkabout', during her tour of New Zealand in March 1970, was to become an expected part of royal engagements as much in Britain as overseas. As an exercise in public relations, the 'walkabout' ranked among the most successful innovations of the reign, for not since the last war, when George VI and his consort established themselves as the people's King and Queen, had the sovereign seemed so accessible.

By the early part of the decade, as will be seen in a moment, the Queen had also learned to laugh at herself when the occasion demanded. Yet while the seventies were to yield a number of joyful royal events, one which occurred very early on not only brought sorrow, but a time for reflection. In May 1972, not quite two weeks after the Queen and Prince Philip had returned to London at the close of their State Visit to Paris as the guests of President Pompidou and the French Government, the Duke of Windsor died of cancer at his home near the Bois de Boulogne. During their visit the royal couple, accompanied by Prince Charles, had called upon the Duke and Duchess at their elegant mansion on the Route du Champ d'Entrainement. The Queen saw the Duke alone in his room before re-joining the Duchess, who, at the age of seventy-six, appeared every bit as chic and handsome as she had almost forty years earlier when, as Mrs Simpson, she and King Edward VIII had monopolized the world's attention, and the drama which led rapidly to the King's abdication unfolded.

At the end of the forty-minute visit, the Duchess of Windsor accompanied her royal guests to their waiting car and, for a moment or two, posed for the group of press photographers assembled on the gravel path. Brief though the Queen's visit had been there was nothing in the cordiality of their farewells to suggest, much less betray, the tragic gulf that had separated the Duke and Duchess from the rest of their family for thirty-six years.

On 5th June the Duke of Windsor, whose body had been flown to England by the Royal Air Force, was accorded a ceremonial funeral at Windsor. But while the service, like the lying-in-state, took place at St George's Chapel—in the presence of the Duchess of Windsor, the Queen and the entire royal family—the man who had been King for less than a year was not interred there along with his sovereign forebears. Instead, he was buried at Frogmore, in the family cemetery

within the shadow of the Mausoleum in which Queen Victoria and the Prince Consort lie entombed.

That the Duke of Windsor continued to be remembered with great affection and respect by vast numbers of ordinary Britons may not have surprised the Duke himself. But doubtless many within court circles were astounded by the warm sentiments his death occasioned and, indeed, by the volume of tributes that were paid so spontaneously to both the Duke and his Duchess.

Five months later the Queen and Prince Philip found themselves showered with tributes when they celebrated their Silver Wedding anniversary. In the House of Lords Earl Jellicoe, the Lord Privy Seal, moved 'That an humble address be presented to Her Majesty and His Royal Highness the Duke of Edinburgh on the occasion of the twenty-fifth anniversary of their wedding, to express the deep gratitude of this

With their two eldest children, the Queen and Prince Philip
set out from Buckingham Palace for the state luncheon at the Guildhall
on their silver wedding anniversary, 20th November 1972.
The royal party are seated in the 1902 State Landau.

House for their contribution to the affairs of the nation and for their unfailing example in public and family life, and to convey every good wish for their continuing happiness.'

Lord Jellicoe went on to say that 'they were living in an age of rapid, almost revolutionary, change and it therefore seemed paradoxical that the monarchy had never been more secure than it was today. The explanation for this seeming paradox was to be found in the shining example which the Royal Family had given of family unity and dedicated service to their fellow countrymen and women).

For the Liberals, Lord Byers told the House that: 'There was no doubt that the way in which the monarchy had adapted itself to the rapidly changing circumstances of the last quarter of a century, while maintaining standards of a high order, had given a confidence and reassurance which had contributed a great deal to Britain's social stability. We are fortunate to have this family at the head of our nation. They are not just royals, they are very human, sympathetic people.'

On Monday, 20th November, the royal wedding anniversary was formally marked by a televised service from Westminster Abbey, at the start of which the Queen and Prince Philip, the Prince of Wales, Princess Anne and the Princes Andrew and Edward processed along the nave (as George VI and the then Princess Elizabeth had in 1947) to the hymn 'Praise, My Soul, the King of Heaven'. On their way to the sacrarium they passed between ranks of High Commissioners and ambassadors, members of Parliament, the order of chivalry, and of the royal households, passed a number of 'ordinary' couples specially invited to the service who were also celebrating silver wedding anniversaries that day, and passed a group of foreign royal guests, including Prince Philip's sisters, Margarita of Hohenlohe-Langenburg and Sophie, Princess George of Hanover, Ex-king Michael of Roumania and his wife Anne, born a princess of Bourbon-Parma, and Ex-king Constantine of the Hellenes with his wife, the former Princess Anne-Marie of Denmark.

The Dean of Westminster opened the service by saying: 'We are here in Westminster Abbey, or in our homes, to join together in thanksgiving to Almighty God for the blessings bestowed upon our gracious Queen Elizabeth and Prince Philip, Duke of Edinburgh in the years of their married life, and for the blessings which have come to each and all of us through their marriage and their lives of service. And now we pray that they may be enriched yet more with heavenly gifts; that they may be so replenished with the grace of God's Holy Spirit

ABOVE: Princess Anne on her most
famous horse 'Doublet'

LEFT: Formal portrait of the Prince of Wales,
in the uniform of the Gordon Highlanders

OVERLEAF: The royal family in Canada
during Jubilee Year 1977.

BELOW: The scene in St Paul's as the Prince of Wales and Lady Diana are married by Dr Robert Runcie, the Archbishop of Canterbury.

BOTTOM: The royal family photographed at Windsor Castle after the christening of the Prince and Princess of Wales's second son Prince Henry, in December 1984.

The scene at the Guildhall as the Queen and Prince Philip toast each other.

that they may always incline to His will and walk in His way; and that their example may lead us all in the paths of faithfulness and self-giving.'

That afternoon at a state luncheon held at the Guildhall, Her Majesty made amusing reference not simply to the royal 'We', but also to an expression that had become so synonymous with the Queen's speeches that the widely impersonated words 'My husband and I', had to be deliberately phased out. Addressing the Lord Mayor of London, however, the Queen said, 'I think everybody really will concede that on this, of all days, I should begin my speech with the words "My husband and I"'. Greeted by gales of laughter, the Queen's remark was followed by more applause when she said, 'We, and by that I mean both of us, are most grateful to you for your generous welcome and for the kind and thoughtful way in which you have expressed the City's loyalty and affection . . .'.

'I must confess', the Queen went on, 'that it came as a bit of a surprise to realise that we had been married for twenty-five years. Neither of us are much given to looking back and the years have slipped by so quickly. Now that we have reached this milestone in our lives we can see how immensely lucky we have been, or perhaps fortunate might be a better word. We had the good fortune to grow up in happy and united families, we have been fortunate in our children and, above all, we are fortunate in being able to serve this great country and Commonwealth.

One year later, almost to the very day, the bells of Westminster Abbey rang out once again in royal celebration, this time for the wedding of the Queen and Prince Philip's only daughter, the twenty-three-year-old Princess Anne. A member of the 'working' royal team since 1969 when, at the age of eighteen, she undertook her first solo official engagement, presenting leeks to the Welsh Guards at Pirbright in Surrey, the Princess enjoyed a popularity that had reached its height by the time her engagement to Captain (then Lieutenant) Mark Phillips of the Queen's Dragoon Guards was announced on 29th May 1973.

Though never possessed of outstanding beauty, Princess Anne was nevertheless a highly attractive girl whose 'debut' on the royal stage generated very considerable interest. Every bit as horse-mad as her mother, Princess Anne took up competitive riding with gusto and entered the Horse of the Year Show at Wembley in 1971, followed by the Badminton Horse Trials and then the Individual Three-Day Event at Burghley, from which she emerged victorious and was subsequently voted Sportswoman, as well as Sports Personality, of the year. (In 1976 Princess Anne and her old friend Richard Meade were to be the only members of the British team to complete the Equestrian Event at the Olympic Games in Canada.)

Horses also had a part to play in the Princess's official life, too, and one of her earliest appointments was as patron of the RDA—Riding for the Disabled Association. It was as President of the Save the Children Fund, however, that Princess Anne was to win loud and justly deserved praise for her tireless work in aid of the underprivileged,

RIGHT: Wedding group: Princess Anne and Mark Philips after their wedding.
They pose in the Throne Room at Buckingham Palace with Captain Eric Grounds, the best man,
Prince Edward and Lady Sarah Armstrong-Jones.

particularly in countries of the Third World. Never one for the meaningless social whirl, encountering the unctuous and sybaritic, Princess Anne preferred to use her position to better advantage and help focus attention on issues of universal importance.

At the close of 1973, 'the winter of our discontent' as some referred to it, Princess Anne's wedding briefly diverted the nation's attention away from something that was about to become a regular feature of the British way of life—industrial unrest.

On the cold, but sunlit, morning of 14th November, which also happened to be Prince Charles's twenty-fifth birthday, 500 million television viewers around the world watched as Princess Anne was cheered on her way to Westminster Abbey by crowds estimated to have been almost 50,000 strong. Travelling with her father in the Glass Coach and followed in two carriages by her bridesmaid, Sarah Armstrong-Jones, her page-boy, Prince Edward, her ladies-in-waiting, Mary Dawnay and Rowena Brassey, and her father's private secretary, William Willett, the royal bride passed along a processional route lined by four regimental bands and nearly 900 troops and officers, drawn from each of the armed services.

As Princess Anne and the Duke of Edinburgh entered the west door of Westminster Abbey, they were welcomed by the Dean of Westminster and the sound of a fanfare played by trumpeters of the bridegroom's regiment. It was a brief pause before the Princess's procession moved off on its four-minute walk towards the high altar, Captain Phillips and his best man, Captain Eric Grounds, but long enough for the television commentators to describe the bride who, it was unanimously agreed, had never looked lovelier. Her wedding gown, designed by Maureen Baker of Susan Small, was of pure ivory silk with a high mandarin collar and pin-tucked bodice. The long, billowing sleeves, which were set over finely pleated undersleeves, gathered at the wrist, were of Tudor inspiration, and the court train, fastened to the shoulders and shimmering with hundreds of mirror jewels and seed pearls, was reminiscent of that worn by the Princess's mother. There was one more reminder of the Queen's wedding, too, in that Princess Anne's full veil of silk tulle was secured by the same diamond tiara borrowed, once again, from Queen Elizabeth The Queen Mother.

For the Queen, dressed that day in sapphire blue, the wedding of her daughter was an especially proud occasion and, at the end of the ceremony, while watching the Princess and her husband drive away to

Buckingham Palace, her delight was unmistakable, especially when, in a spontaneous moment of excitement, she was seen bobbing up and down on her heels.

Scarcely had Princess Anne slipped from the front pages of the national press than she and Captain Phillips were thrust dramatically back into the headlines.

Wednesday, 20th March 1974, had been pretty much a routine day for the Princess when in the early evening, she and her husband, attended by Rowena Brassey, climbed into an elderly Austin Princess limousine waiting for them at the King's Door which led out into the Inner Quadrangle at Buckingham Palace. Above the windscreen an heraldic shield, bearing the Princess's coat-of-arms, was illuminated, while below it a small blue light—found on nearly all official royal cars—was put on. This helps police on point duty to recognize the approach of royal limousines. The couple's destination that night was Newgate Street in the City, where they were to attend a private showing of a film made by the Riding for the Disabled Association and which, given the event about to unfold, was ironically called *Riding Towards Freedom*.

The engagement passed off without incident until shortly after 8 p.m. Then, as the royal car neared St James's Palace on its return journey along the Mall, a Ford Escort driven by a man later identified as Ian Ball suddenly accelerated, overtook the limousine and, swerving in front of it, forced it to stop. Armed with a pistol, Ball abandoned his car and ran towards Princess Anne firing a volley of shots through the near-side door and windows of the Austin. Detective-Inspector James Beaton, the Princess's detective, fired a single shot from his Walther PP automatic before it jammed and the gunman wounded him in the chest and arms. Then the Princess's chauffeur, Alex Callender, slumped over the steering wheel, a bullet lodged in his chest. Within seconds, Police-Constable Michael Hills, who had run across from St James's Palace, was also felled, shot in the liver, while a stray bullet struck the passenger of a passing taxi.

Miss Sammy Scott, who gave an eye-witness account of the shooting, said: 'I saw a woman in a pink dress getting out of the car. I presumed that it was Princess Anne's lady-in-waiting. She crouched down by the side of the car. I ran to her and asked what was happening. She shouted at me "Get down. There's a maniac loose." A man . . . was

trying to get into the royal car. He was shaking the door madly and firing wildly at the car. I could see Princess Anne and Mark huddled in the back. Then they tried to get out by the opposite door, but the gunman rushed round and started trying to get in that side, still firing his pistol. Just then about six policemen leapt on him.'

At Buckingham Palace within half an hour of the drama, the Princess and her husband, though severely shaken gave a full statement of the incident to the head of the Royalty Protection Squad. Speaking later that night, Princess Anne expressed her concern for those who had been wounded. 'We are very thankful to be in one piece,' she said, 'but we are deeply concerned about those who got injured.

'Inspector Beaton acted particularly bravely and although already shot he continued to protect us. We are extremely grateful to all those members of the police and public who tried to help us.'

In Indonesia, where they were on a five-day visit, the Queen and Prince Philip were woken before dawn to be given the news from London. Both were 'horrified at the incident, but are relieved . . . that no one was killed.'

Ian Ball, whose plan had been to kidnap Princess Anne and hold her to a £1,000,000 ransom, was jailed indefinitely.

Though few events were as disturbing or outrageous as the one-man ambush in the Mall, royal family events continued apace for the rest of the decade. In March 1976 the tragic futility of Princess Margaret and Lord Snowdon's marriage finally led to separation and the release of a formal statement which read: 'HRH The Princess Margaret, Countess of Snowdon and the Earl of Snowdon have mutually agreed to live apart. The Princess will carry out her public duties and functions unaccompanied by Lord Snowdon. There are no plans for divorce proceedings.'

The Snowdon marriage had been a source of gossip and rumour for several years and more than once had it been openly discussed on the front pages. But what was not generally known was that the prophecies of disaster, given voice at the time of the couple's wedding, had already begun to ring true as early as 1964 and cracks of widening discord had been repaired, at least cosmetically, on a number of occasions thereafter. By the time the couple finally faced official separation Princess Margaret and her husband had, in fact, been leading separate

lives, albeit under the same roof, for some considerable time. Yet while the formal dissolution of their marriage was not contemplated in March 1976, chiefly because Princess Margaret did not approve of divorce, it was only to be a matter of time before a petition was submitted to the London Divorce Court. Indeed, two years later, on 24th May 1978, the Snowdons' suit—along with twenty-seven other cases—appeared before Judge Roger Willis. 'Is there any party or any person present to show cause why a decree should not be pronounced?' he asked the court. When there was no reply, Judge Willis declared, 'Very well, I pronounce decree nisi in accordance with the respective Registrars' certificates.'

Alternately 'horrified' and 'saddened' by the issues we have just looked at, the Queen must surely have been glad that her Silver Jubilee held in prospect an occasion for celebration, one that would, in any event, train the spotlight of publicity away from the supporting cast and back to the single most important character in the on-going saga of the family Windsor.

The actual twenty-fifth anniversary of the Queen's accession—Sunday, 6th February 1977—was observed, as may have been

Sunday, 6th February 1977, the twenty-fifth anniversary of Her Majesty's accession. Here the Queen and other members of her family greet the Dean of Windsor after morning service at the Royal Chapel of All Saints on the Royal Lodge estate, Windsor.

expected, simply and quietly. For all that that day represented a significant milestone in Her Majesty's life, it wasn't to be forgotten that it also represented the twenty-fifth anniversary of her father's death. That morning the Queen was joined for the usual morning service at the Royal Chapel of All Saints in Windsor Great Park by Prince Philip, Queen Elizabeth The Queen Mother, Prince Charles, Princess Anne, Prince Edward and Princess Margaret. The more flamboyant and national act of thanksgiving for the Queen's reign was reserved for Tuesday, 7th June.

Throughout the summer of 1977 some 300 major events had been organized to mark the Silver Jubilee in Great Britain, and the Queen herself was scheduled to take part in a great many of them. In May, for instance, Her Majesty launched HMS *Invincible* at Barrow-in-Furness, received Loyal Addresses from both Houses of Parliament at Westminster Hall, reviewed a parade of Silver Ghost Rolls-Royce cars at Windsor Castle, received 'Centennial', a horse presented to her four years earlier by the Commissioner of the Royal Canadian Mounted Police, and attended Scotland's formal programme of events, including a national service of thanksgiving at Glasgow Cathedral.

Later on in London, a gala evening of opera and ballet was staged at the Royal Opera House to which Her Majesty was accompanied by nearly every member of her family, and nine days later, they witnessed a magnificent river pageant and firework display on the Thames. That night, incidentally, delighted revellers not only witnessed the picturesque, and extremely rare, spectacle of a night-time royal procession, as the Queen and members of the royal family returned to Buckingham Palace in the fleet of state carriages, candles flickering in each of the highly-polished lanterns, but cheered to the echo when Her Majesty made a midnight appearance on the balcony of the floodlit palace.

Not all the Jubilee events could proudly speak of royal visitors, but some were sufficiently memorable for all that. The Victoria & Albert Museum, for example, mounted an opulent exhibition of works by Carl Fabergé, court jeweller to the last Russian imperial family; *Lousy but Loyal*, a photographic exhibition showed how London's eastenders had celebrated past jubilees; *Royal Box* was designed as a pictorial and musical celebration of royalty and the theatre; and *A Garland for the Queen* brought a 1953 coronation musical back to London.

Jubilee Day itself, despite the cold, wet weather, saw a million people enjoying the pageantry of the state procession from Buck-

A loyal gesture from the London cab trade—a silver London taxi,
driven by Prince Charles in the Inner Quadrangle at Buckingham
Palace—bearing the 1977 Silver Jubilee emblem on its door.

ingham Palace to St Paul's Cathedral. Indeed, by 3 a.m. on 7th June,
discovering a front-row place anywhere along the Mall was akin to
striking gold! All through the night good-humoured crowds, wrapped
in blankets and sleeping-bags, reminisced about past royal occasions,
opened picnic baskets and hold-alls containing refreshments, furled
and unfurled umbrellas when the heavens opened and raised their feet
as the rainwater gushed along the gutters.

At 10.25 a.m. the first of three processions left Buckingham Palace.
Riding in seven state landaus and accompanied by a Captain's Escort
of the Household Cavalry were Princess Anne and Captain Mark
Phillips, Princess Margaret, Princess Alice, Duchess of Gloucester,
Viscount Linley and Lady Sarah Armstrong-Jones, the Duke and

ABOVE: The scene inside St Paul's Cathedral during the Jubilee service of thanksgiving.

LEFT: Former prime ministers Wilson and Heath sit in front of Gough Whitlam, Australian prime minister, and his wife.

TOWARDS THE FUTURE

Duchess of Gloucester, the Duke and Duchess of Kent with their sons George, Earl of St Andrews, and Lord Nicholas Windsor, and their daughter Lady Helen, Princess Alexandra with the Honourable Angus Ogilvy, their son James and their daughter Marina, and lastly Prince Michael of Kent with Earl Mountbatten of Burma.

Ten minutes later, to a rousing reception, came Queen Elizabeth The Queen Mother, driving with Prince Andrew and Prince Edward in the delicate Scottish State Coach. Then, of course, came the Queen herself, dressed in a soft pink outfit and travelling at walking pace in the vast State Coach which, as one observer put it, 'swayed slightly from side to side, like some great gilded galleon'.

The service in St Paul's Cathedral was as impressive as any of its kind in the past and clearly, one specially composed prayer, reverently punctuated with thees, thous and thys, was specifically intended to capture the essence of the occasion, even if, in part, its heady exultations painted a picture of a sovereign more suited to the middle ages than the 1970s:

> Almighty God, who rulest over all kingdoms of the world, and dost order them accordingly to Thy good pleasure,' intoned the Dean of St Paul's solemnly, 'We yield Thee humble, hearty thanks, because Thou, hast set Thy Servant our Sovereign Lady, Queen Elizabeth, upon the throne of this Realm.
>
> 'We bless and praise Thee that, in all things, Thy wisdom is her guide; that in all things thine arm doth strengthen her; that she, knowing whose minister she is, doth ever seek Thy honour and glory and study to preserve Thy people committed to her charge that people of every nation and kindred and tongue are strengthened and inspired by her faith in Thee, by her devotion to the welfare of all mankind.'

At the end of the hour-long service, the Queen stepped out into the real world of the twentieth-century once more and, with Prince Philip, the Lord Mayor of London and the Lady Mayoress, walked the short distance to the Guildhall for the state luncheon given in her honour. By 3.30 that afternoon the royal party had returned to Buckingham Palace and an hour later, with the balcony appearances over and the pomp and splendour of another full-scale occasion behind them, the Queen and Prince Philip were able to change into more casual clothing and put their feet up for a while.

At the start of Jubilee year the Queen and Prince Philip had made tours of Western Samoa, Fiji, Tonga, Papua New Guinea, Australia

From the royal yacht *Britannia*, the Queen and the royal party
witness the Jubilee Review at Spithead.

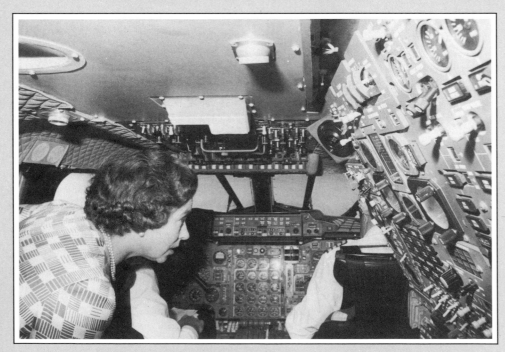

Returning from a Jubilee tour of the West Indies, the Queen
inspects the controls on the flight-deck of Concorde.

and New Zealand to receive the good wishes of the Commonwealth, and in October the royal couple left Britain to wind up their official obligations in Canada, the Bahamas, Antigua, British Virgin Islands and Barbados. Yet no matter how warm the welcome given to the Queen on her travels that autumn, none could have been warmer than that which the Queen herself accorded her first grandchild soon after her return to London.

It was shortly before 4 a.m. on Tuesday, 15th November, the day after her fourth wedding anniversary, when Princess Anne was driven to St Mary's Hospital in Paddington, by her husband. Seven hours later, a statement signed by the royal gynaecologist announced, 'The Princess Anne, Mrs Mark Phillips was safely delivered of a son ... at 10.46 a.m. today. Her Royal Highness and her son are both doing well.'

From the Tower of London the birth of Master Peter Phillips, who had weighed in at 7 lb 9 oz, was greeted by a forty-one-gun salute, fired by the Honourable Artillery Company, and that evening the Queen, 'smiling radiantly' to coin one of Fleet Street's favourite clichés, spent half an hour at St Mary's with her daughter and grandson.

That morning, in fact, the news had reached the Queen shortly before the start of an investiture in the ballroom at Buckingham Palace. Arriving ten minutes late, Her Majesty told the assembled company, 'I apologize for being late, but I have just had a message from the hospital. My daughter has just given birth to a son and I am now a grandmother.' At the end of the lengthy ceremony, during which the recipients of honours extended their personal congratulations, the Queen retired from the ballroom to renewed applause and the sound of the string band of the Scots Guards playing *Happy Birthday*.

Little more than seven months after the birth of Princess Anne's son, a particularly interesting royal wedding introduced the nation to a new Princess and provided the royal family with its first intake of fresh air for a very long time. What made this marriage quite so interesting was the fact that Prince Michael of Kent, younger son of the late Prince George, Duke of Kent and Princess Marina (and on the 'royal' side, one of the Queen's six surviving first cousins), had relinquished his right of inheritance—in accordance with the Act of Settlement 1701—

A more personal Jubilee gift for Her Majesty. On 15th November
1977, Princess Anne gave birth to a son Peter and the Queen
became a grandmother for the first time.

One of the most interesting royal weddings this century was that of the Queen's cousin,
Prince Michael of Kent, to the beautiful Baroness Marie Christine von Reibnitz.
They were married in Vienna on 30th June 1978.

so that he could marry Baroness Marie Christine von Reibnitz, a young woman who was not only a Roman Catholic but also a divorcée.

Prince Michael and the Bohemian-born Baroness had first met during her brief marriage to Tom Troubridge, a young merchant banker and, like the Prince himself, an old Etonian. In an interview Princess Michael gave to the present author in 1984 she explained how a casual friendship with the Prince first developed. 'He was a charming spare man I used to invite to dinner parties or when I had extremely eligible European relatives over', Her Royal Highness said. 'I thought, this young man is all alone; I'll produce the right girl-friend for him. I saw myself as a sort of fairy-godmother, waving my magic wand.'

The end of the Princess's first marriage, however, meant that the 'spell' her 'wand' had cast over Prince Michael himself soon became manifest and before long, Lord Mountbatten told the Princess, 'You ought to marry that young man.' 'Why?' she asked. 'Because he's madly in love with you.' At that point, Princess Michael explained, 'I sat up and looked again. I had never thought of it really, because there was I a foreigner, Catholic and divorced. I was convinced it was out of the question.'

Though the couple's circumstances did prove difficult, and while frustration and bitter disappointment lay in store for them, Prince and Princess Michael of Kent were married in a civil ceremony in Vienna, attended by Princess Anne, the Duke of Kent, Princess Alexandra and Lord Mountbatten, on 30th June 1978. Five years later the Roman Catholic Church formally recognized the marriage and, to the Princess's especial delight, she and Prince Michael were permitted a Ceremony of Validation, which was celebrated privately in London, at Archbishop's House, a part of Westminster Cathedral, on 29th July 1983.

If the 1960s had all but ended on a colourful note, the seventies were to close on a tragically misguided act of terrorism, one that deprived the Queen and Prince Philip of a dearly loved friend and uncle and, indeed, robbed the Prince of Wales, as well as Prince and Princess Michael of Kent, of a wise and influential mentor.

Lord Mountbatten's assassination by the IRA occurred on Bank Holiday Monday, 27th August 1979, when his yacht *Shadow V* was blown up by a remote-controlled bomb off the coast of County Sligo, near Mullaghmore. It was an ignoble end to the life of a man for whom

even total strangers held a strong affection. Indeed, this was something most of his obituaries remarked upon. The *Illustrated London News* in its special tribute said, in part, 'In all he did in a long and active life Mountbatten successfully combined qualities of leadership, which were partly inherited and in part assiduously cultivated, with an enthusiasm, charm and courtesy that won him a host of devoted friends throughout the world and many more admirers among people he had never met but who nonetheless recognized and respected in him the virtues of a hero.'

Like 'Dickie' Mountbatten, Queen Elizabeth The Queen Mother has always had a particularly strong influence over the affairs of her family. And although Her Majesty's image has consistently appeared to be as light-weight as the silk chiffons in which she is frequently swathed, there is behind it all a woman of very considerable force and determination, one who is regarded by many who know her well as 'an iron fist in a velvet glove'. It is, however, the combination of sheer professionalism and devotion to duty, coloured overall by a certain lightness of touch, that has endeared her to untold millions throughout a career that has now spanned more than sixty years.

On 4th August 1980 Queen Elizabeth celebrated her eightieth birthday by attending a special gala ballet performance at the Royal Opera House, accompanied by the Queen and members of her immediate family. A short time before, on 15th July, a national tribute to the Queen Mother took the form of a thanksgiving service at St Paul's Cathedral. Yet although no Queen Dowager had ever been honoured in this way before it was stressed beforehand that this was not a state occasion. On the day itself amid all the pomp and circumstance of trumpet fanfares, carriage processions and Cavalry escorts, one could have been forgiven for thinking otherwise.

That autumn at a belated party held at the Ritz to celebrate another family birthday—Princess Margaret's fiftieth—a royal romance that had been subject to rumour and speculation for several weeks, was fast approaching the point of no return. Now retired from a naval 'career', considered by some courtiers to have been of little real benefit, the Prince of Wales found himself under pressure to take a wife before time, and the already worrying shortage of acceptable candidates, finally ran out.

With a little careful stage-managing on the part of the family, Lady

The Queen with the Queen Mother, Prince Philip and Prince Edward
arrive at St Paul's on 29th July 1981 for the marriage of the
Prince of Wales and Lady Diana Spencer.

Diana Spencer, nineteen-year-old daughter of Earl Spencer, a former royal equerry, was deemed the most promising contender and, at the end of February 1981, the couple's engagement was formally announced.

From that moment on, although it was a far from enviable prospect, 'Lady Di', as the media called her, stood poised to become all things to all men: a possible future Queen for England, a 'Dynasty'-style model girl front for the royal House of Windsor, a dream-come-true for the popular press, the hairdressing fraternity and the manufacturers of dresses, coats, suits and evening wear, hats, shoes and stockings; chatelaine of a mansion in Gloucestershire called Highgrove and two sizeable houses converted into one at Kensington Palace, and, in due course, the mother of a new heir-presumptive. Few, if any, young women in the public eye had ever been subject to such massive over-exposure, but if it is true that Lady Diana's youthful ambition was to become either a ballet-dancer or the Princess of Wales, then perhaps she was already ripe for 'stardom'.

In those early days, however, few could have guessed that the demure Lady Diana concealed behind her shy smile an enormously strong will that would not only cause the Queen and Prince Charles some anxious moments, but would, before long, send from their Household several members of staff, including two Private Secretaries. One of them, the Honourable Edward Adeane, could look back to the time of Queen Victoria to find his great-grandfather serving the legendary sovereign in the same capacity.

It soon became clear that as Princess of Wales (or 'Princess Diana', as she is erroneously called), the Queen's daughter-in-law fully intended to do things her way. 'I still believe that the Princess is trying to retain some of her own identity, which is not simple if you marry a Royal', wrote Stephen Barry, former valet to Prince Charles. 'It's very easy to be submerged and become thoroughly miserable.'

The royal wedding, celebrated on 29th July 1981 at St Paul's Cathedral—and not at Westminster Abbey, as most had expected—was nothing if not an occasion for jubilation. Though arguably marred to some extent by excessive ostentation, which tended to exaggerate the importance of the event, it nevertheless drew people together—in much the same way as the Queen's Silver Jubilee had done four years earlier—and left in the minds of all who saw it colourful images of one of the most memorable pageants this century. In the streets the crowds numbered somewhere between 600,000 and 900,000 while British

Prince Andrew and Princess Anne, participants in a Charity All-Star Shooting competition, 1984.

television alone claimed 39 million viewers. By the time the Prince and Princess of Wales were driving back to Buckingham Palace in the scarlet and gold 1902 State Landau, television was claiming its biggest success ever, with world-wide viewing figures—the wedding was beamed 'live' to seventy-four countries via 109 television services—standing at a staggering 750 million.

At the time of her Silver Jubilee, the Queen could hardly have guessed that only five years later HMS *Invincible*, which she had just launched, would be carrying her second son off to war. In April 1982, however, that is exactly what happened when Argentinian forces invaded the Falkland Islands in the South Atlantic, and Britain

despatched her task force to rout the marauders and re-establish her long-held, if long-disputed, sovereignty.

At the age of twenty-two, Prince Andrew was among the helicopter pilots of 820 Sea King Squadron aboard the *Invincible*. For the Queen—as for any other parent—the conflict was a nightmare of anxiety and, in common with the rest of her family, awaited every scrap of news with an anguish that belied her usual surface calm. Prince Andrew was, in fact, the first British Prince to have seen combat

Prince Andrew and some of his naval colleagues returning from the Falklands in 1982.

since his father distinguished himself at the Battle of Cape Matapan during the Second World War and, indeed, the young Prince's own record in the South Atlantic was to prove no less outstanding.

The most personable and down-to-earth of all the royal menfolk, Prince Andrew was determined that his own service career should follow exactly the same lines as those of his colleagues, with no special privileges because of his royal rank. Thus in the Falklands Prince Andrew gave no thought to his own life or safety when under attack or when his helicopter was used as a decoy for the lethal Exocet missile.

Later a fellow officer said, 'One of the most refreshing aspects of Prince Andrew's personality is the candour and honesty which made him unashamed to admit to fear. A hero, most of the time, is an ordinary man who keeps perfectly natural fears under control, accepting risks as part of a sense of duty, but well aware of their nature nevertheless.'

Britain's victory gave rise to as much relief within the royal family as in any other where sons had survived what is known as the South Atlantic Campaign. That summer, too, an altogether different kind of event occasioned further happiness and celebration—the birth of a son, William, on 21st June, to the Prince and Princess of Wales. Both were proud moments for the Queen and Prince Philip and that pride was compounded still further on 15th September 1984 when a second son, 'Harry', was born to the Prince and Princess. Indeed with an interest in the royal family line that is every bit as acute as that of her great-great-grandmother Queen Victoria, Her Majesty might well have been reminded of a letter the great Queen wrote to her eldest daughter Vicky, the Empress Frederick of Germany, in June 1894. Then, when remarking on the birth of a grandson—who was to end his life as the Duke of Windsor—Queen Victoria enthused ' . . . it seems that it has never happened in this Country that there shd be three direct Heirs as well as the Sovereign alive'.

As the Queen celebrates her sixtieth birthday—an anniversary which must so surely represent an important milestone in the life of any individual—Her Majesty may just pause to reflect on some of the events that have passed in her own life and in that of her family. She may also stop to consider the changes she has seen in the progress of the monarchy itself, many of which she has made to help bring the institution she personifies more in line with today.

The demands upon the sovereign have not diminished over the years, but have become rather more intense. So, indeed, have the

dangers that attend the lives of all public figures in these uncertain times. We think, for instance, of the attack made upon Princess Anne in 1974, of the unfortunate youth whose quest to become noticed led him to fire blank shots at the Queen as she rode to the Trooping the Colour ceremony in 1981, and of the remarkable episode of the intruder who found his way into Her Majesty's bedroom at Buckingham Palace little more than a year later. Yet come what may, it is clear that the Queen herself prefers to adopt an optimistic point of view. 'I feel that in the world today there is too much concentration on the gloomy side of life, so that we tend to underestimate our blessings', she has said.

In choosing a title for this study it was decided to borrow a popular phrase from the time of Queen Victoria's Diamond Jubilee. In 1897, however, the celebratory tone of the words 'Sixty Glorious Years' proposed a toast to the achievements of an era as much as to the reign of the sovereign herself. Today, those same words are reiterated here in celebration of the *life* and achievements of Her Majesty Queen Elizabeth II.

SELECT BIBLIOGRAPHY

Andrew Duncan	*The Reality of Monarchy* (Heinemann, 1970)
Olwen Hedley	*The Queen's Silver Jubilee* (Pitkin, 1976)
Robert Lacey	*Majesty—Elizabeth II and The House of Windsor* (Hutchinson & Co Ltd, 1977)
Peter Lane	*Prince Philip* (Robert Hale, 1980)
Elizabeth Longford	*Elizabeth R* (Weidenfeld & Nicolson, 1983)
Ann Morrow	*The Queen* (Granada, 1983)
Christopher Warwick	*King George VI & Queen Elizabeth* (Sidgwick & Jackson, 1985)
Christopher Warwick	*Princess Margaret* (Weidenfeld & Nicolson, 1983)
Christopher Warwick	*Two Centuries of Royal Weddings* (Arthur Barker, 1980)

The *Illustrated London News*
The Times
The *Daily Telegraph*
Majesty—The Monthly Royal Review

ACKNOWLEDGEMENTS

The publishers would like to thank the following for supplying illustrations:

COLOUR

John Scott *25, 26, 27, 28, 109 (above), 111, 112, 129, 130 (above), 131 (above), 132, 149, 150, 152*; Charles Stokes *109 (below), 110 (left), 131 (below)*

BLACK AND WHITE

BBC Hulton Picture Library *72, 80, 86 (below)*; Central Press Photos *19, 33, 37, 52, 57, 60, 66, 77 (above), 81, 86 (above), 117, 121, 122, 139, 140, 166*; Fox Photos *13, 59, 73, 74, 75, 89, 92, 101, 104, 108, 114, 118, 123, 127, 135, 136, 138, 147, 153, 155, 159, 161, 162, 164 (above)*; Keystone Press Agency *6, 8, 29, 31, 32, 36, 57, 67, 102, 105, 106, 115, 125, 133, 140, 142, 164 (below), 167, 170, 172, 173*; National Portrait Gallery *44, 48, 49, 51, 56, 66, 68, 70, 77 (below), 84, 90*; Photographic News Agencies *97*; Press Photo Combine *175*; Syndication International *63*